Modigliani: 90 Paintings

Paintings&Drawings, Volume 4

Jessica Findley

Published by Icon-m, 2014.

MODIGLIANI: 90 PAINTINGS

First edition. November 26, 2014.

Written by Jessica Findley.

Also by Jessica Findley

Paintings&Drawings
Egon Schiele: Paintings and Drawings
Modigliani: 90 Paintings

Standalone
Camille Corot: 130 Paintings
Antoine Watteau: 78 Paintings

Foreword

Amedeo Clemente Modigliani (July 12, 1884 – January 24, 1920) was an Italian painter and sculptor who worked mainly in France. Primarily a figurative artist, he became known for paintings and sculptures in a modern style characterized by mask-like faces and elongation of form. He died in Paris of tubercular meningitis, exacerbated by poverty, overwork and addiction to alcohol and narcotics.

Modigliani was born into a Jewish family in Livorno, Italy. A port city, Livorno had long served as a refuge for those persecuted for their religion, and was home to a large Jewish community. His maternal great-great-grandfather, Solomon Garsin, had immigrated to Livorno in the 18th century as a refugee.

Modigliani's mother (Eugénie Garsin) who was born and grew up in Marseille, was descended from an intellectual, scholarly family of Sephardic Jews, generations of whom had resided along the Mediterranean coastline. Her ancestors were learned people, fluent in many languages, known authorities on sacred Jewish texts and founders of a school of Talmudic studies. Family legend traced the Garsins' lineage to the 17th-century Dutch philosopher Baruch Spinoza.

The family business was believed to be a credit agency with branches in Livorno, Marseille, Tunis, and London. Their financial fortunes ebbed and flowed. At times they enjoyed affluence, at other times they were subject to dire financial crises and reduced circumstances.

Modigliani's father, Flaminio, hailed from a family of successful businessmen and entrepreneurs. While not as culturally sophisticated as the Garsins, they knew how to invest into and develop thriving business endeavors. Their wealth was derived from mining the metals abundant in the area of Sardinia and Tuscany and extracting and exporting the ores. When the Garsin and Modigliani families announced the engagement of their children, Flaminio was a wealthy young mining engineer. He managed the mine in Sardinia and oversaw the almost 30,000 acres of timberland the family owned. He also was expert in both forestry and farming management. A reversal in fortune occurred to this prosperous family in 1883. An economic downturn in the price of metal plunged the Modiglianis into bankruptcy. Ever resourceful, Modigliani's mother used her social contacts to establish a school and, along with her two sisters, made the school into a successful enterprise.

Modigliani was the fourth child, whose birth coincided with the disastrous financial collapse of his father's business interests. Amedeo's birth saved the family from ruin; according to an ancient law, creditors could not seize the bed of a pregnant woman or a mother with a newborn child. The bailiffs entered the family's home just as Eugenia went into labor; the family protected their most valuable assets by piling them on top of her.

Modigliani had a close relationship with his mother, who taught him at home until he was 10. Beset with health problems after an attack of pleurisy when he was about 11, a few years later he developed a case of typhoid fever. When he was 16 he was taken ill again and contracted the tuberculosis which would later claim his life. After Modigliani recovered from the second bout of pleurisy, his mother took him on a tour of southern Italy: Naples, Capri, Rome and Amalfi, then north to Florence and Venice.

Modigliani worked in Micheli's Art School from 1898 to 1900. Here his earliest formal artistic instruction took place in an atmosphere steeped in a study of the styles and themes of 19th-century Italian art. In his earliest Parisian work, traces of this influence, and that of his studies of Renaissance art, can still be seen. His nascent work was shaped as much by such artists as Giovanni Boldini as by Toulouse-Lautrec.

Modigliani showed great promise while with Micheli, and ceased his studies only when he was forced to, by the onset of tuberculosis.

In 1901, whilst in Rome, Modigliani admired the work of Domenico Morelli, a painter of melodramatic religious and literary scenes. Morelli had served as an inspiration for a group of iconoclasts who were known by the title "the Macchiaioli" (from macchia —"dash of colour", or, more derogatively, "stain"), and Modigliani had already been exposed to the influences of the Macchiaioli.

This localized landscape movement reacted against the bourgeois styling of the academic genre painters. While sympathetically connected to (and actually pre-dating) the French Impressionists, the Macchiaioli did not make the same impact upon international art culture as did the contemporaries and followers of Monet, and are today largely forgotten outside of Italy.

Modigliani's connection with the movement was through Guglielmo Micheli, his first art teacher. Micheli was not only a Macchiaiolo himself, but had been a pupil of the famous Giovanni Fattori, a founder of the movement. Micheli's work, however, was so fashionable and the genre so commonplace that the young Modigliani reacted against it, preferring to ignore the obsession with landscape that, as with French Impressionism, characterized the movement. Micheli also tried to encourage his pupils to paint en plein air, but Modigliani never really got a taste for this style of working, sketching in cafés, but preferring to paint indoors, and especially in his own studio. Even when compelled to paint landscapes (three are known to exist), Modigliani chose a proto-Cubist palette more akin to Cézanne than to the Macchiaioli.

While with Micheli, Modigliani studied not only landscape, but also portraiture, still life, and the nude. His fellow students recall that the last was where he displayed his greatest talent, and apparently this was not an entirely academic pursuit for the teenager: when not painting nudes, he was occupied with seducing the household maid.

Despite his rejection of the Macchiaioli approach, Modigliani nonetheless found favor with his teacher, who referred to him as "Superman", a pet name reflecting the fact that Modigliani was not only quite adept at his art, but also that he regularly quoted from Nietzsche's Thus Spoke Zarathustra. Fattori himself would often visit the studio, and approved of the young artist's innovations.

In 1902, Modigliani continued what was to be a lifelong infatuation with life drawing, enrolling in the Accademia di Belle Arti (Scuola Libera di Nudo, or "Free School of Nude Studies") in Florence. A year later while still suffering from tuberculosis, he moved to Venice, where he registered to study at the Istituto di Belle Arti.

It is in Venice that he first smoked hashish and, rather than studying, began to spend time frequenting disreputable parts of the city. The impact of these lifestyle choices upon his developing artistic style is open to conjecture, although these choices do seem to be more than simple teenage rebellion, or the hedonism and bohemianism that was almost expected of artists of the time; his pursuit of the seedier side of life appears to have roots in his appreciation of radical philosophies, including those of Nietzsche.

Having been exposed to erudite philosophical literature as a young boy under the tutelage of Isaco Garsin, his maternal grandfather, he continued to read and be influenced through his art studies by the writings of Nietzsche, Baudelaire, Carducci, Comte de Lautréamont, and others, and developed the belief that the only route to true creativity was through defiance and disorder.

Letters that he wrote from his 'sabbatical' in Capri in 1901 clearly indicate that he is being more and more influenced by the thinking of Nietzsche The work of Lautréamont was equally influential at this time. This doomed poet's Les Chants de Maldoror became the seminal work for the Parisian Surrealists of Modigliani's generation, and the book became Modigliani's favorite to the extent that he learnt it by heart.The poetry of Lautréamont is characterized by the juxtaposition of fantastical elements, and by sadistic imagery; the fact that Modigliani was so taken by this text in his early teens gives a good indication of his developing tastes. Baudelaire and D'Annunzio similarly appealed to the young artist, with their interest in corrupted beauty, and the expression of that insight through Symbolist imagery.

Modigliani wrote to Ghiglia extensively from Capri, where his mother had taken him to assist in his recovery from tuberculosis. These letters are a sounding board for the developing ideas brewing in Modigliani's mind.

Ghiglia was seven years Modigliani's senior, and it is likely that it was he who showed the young man the limits of his horizons in Livorno. Like all precocious teenagers, Modigliani preferred the company of older companions, and Ghiglia's role in his adolescence was to be a sympathetic ear as he worked himself out, principally in the convoluted letters that he regularly sent, and which survive today.

"Dear friend, I write to pour myself out to you and to affirm myself to myself. I am the prey of great powers that surge forth and then disintegrate...A bourgeois told me today – insulted me – that I or at least my brain was lazy. It did me good. I should like such a warning every morning upon awakening: but they cannot understand us nor can they understand life..."

In 1906, Modigliani moved to Paris, then the focal point of the avant-garde. In fact, his arrival at the centre of artistic experimentation coincided with the arrival of two other foreigners who were also to leave their marks upon the art world: Gino Severini and Juan Gris.

He settled in Le Bateau-Lavoir, a commune for penniless artists in Montmartre, renting himself a studio in Rue Caulaincourt. Even though this artists' quarter of Montmartre was characterized by generalized poverty, Modigliani himself presented — initially, at least — as one would expect the son of a family trying to

maintain the appearances of its lost financial standing to present:
his wardrobe was dapper without ostentation, and the studio he
rented was appointed in a style appropriate to someone with a
finely attuned taste in plush drapery and Renaissance
reproductions.

He soon made efforts to assume the guise of the bohemian
artist, but, even in his brown corduroys, scarlet scarf and large
black hat, he continued to appear as if he were slumming it, having
fallen upon harder times.

When he first arrived in Paris, he wrote home regularly to his
mother, he sketched his nudes at the Académie Colarossi, and he
drank wine in moderation. He was at that time considered by
those who knew him as a bit reserved, verging on the asocial. He is
noted to have commented, upon meeting Picasso who, at the time,
was wearing his trademark workmen's clothes, that even though
the man was a genius that did not excuse his uncouth appearance.

Within a year of arriving in Paris, however, his demeanour and
reputation had changed dramatically. He transformed himself
from a dapper academician artist into a sort of prince of
vagabonds.

The poet and journalist Louis Latourette, upon visiting the
artist's previously well-appointed studio after his transformation,
discovered the place in upheaval, the Renaissance reproductions
discarded from the walls, the plush drapes in disarray. Modigliani
was already an alcoholic and a drug addict by this time, and his
studio reflected this. Modigliani's behavior at this time sheds some
light upon his developing style as an artist, in that the studio had
become almost a sacrificial effigy for all that he resented about the
academic art that had marked his life and his training up to that
point.

Not only did he remove all the trappings of his bourgeois
heritage from his studio, but he also set about destroying
practically all of his own early work. He explained this
extraordinary course of actions to his astonished neighbors thus:

The motivation for this violent rejection of his earlier self is the subject of considerable speculation. From the time of his arrival in Paris, Modigliani consciously crafted a charade persona for himself and cultivated his reputation of hopeless drunk and voracious drug user. His escalating intake of drugs and alcohol may have been a means by which Modigliani masked his tuberculosis from his acquaintances, few of whom knew of his condition. Tuberculosis — the leading cause of death in France by 1900 — was highly communicable, there was no cure, and those who had it were feared, ostracized, and pitied. Modigliani thrived on camaraderie and would not let himself be isolated as an invalid; he sought to suppress his coughing bouts and any other recognizable signs of the disease that was slowly consuming him. Modigliani used drink and drugs to self-medicate, to serve as palliatives to ease his physical pain, helping him to maintain a facade of vitality and allowing him to continue to create his art.

Modigliani's use of drink and drugs intensified from about 1914 onward. After years of remission and recurrence, this was the period in when the symptoms of his tuberculosis worsened, signaling that the disease had reached an advanced stage.

He sought the company of artists such as Utrillo and Soutine, seeking acceptance and validation for his work from his colleagues. Modigliani's behavior stood out even in these Bohemian surroundings: he carried on frequent affairs, drank heavily, and used absinthe and hashish. While drunk, he would sometimes strip himself naked at social gatherings. He became the epitome of the tragic artist, creating a posthumous legend almost as well known as that of Vincent van Gogh.

During his early years in Paris, Modigliani worked at a furious pace. He was constantly sketching, making as many as a hundred drawings a day. However, many of his works were lost — destroyed by him as inferior, left behind in his frequent changes of address, or given to girlfriends who did not keep them.

He was first influenced by Henri de Toulouse-Lautrec, but around 1907 he became fascinated with the work of Paul Cézanne. Eventually he developed his own unique style, one that cannot be adequately categorized with those of other artists.

He met the first serious love of his life, Russian poet Anna Akhmatova, in 1910, when he was 26. They had studios in the same building, and although 21-year-old Anna was recently married, they began an affair. Anna was tall (as Modigliani was only 5 foot 5 inches) with dark hair (like Modigliani's), pale skin and grey-green eyes, she embodied Modigliani's aesthetic ideal and the pair became engrossed in each other. After a year, however, Anna returned to her husband.

In 1909, Modigliani returned home to Livorno, sickly and tired from his wild lifestyle. Soon he was back in Paris, this time renting a studio in Montparnasse. He originally saw himself as a sculptor rather than a painter, and was encouraged to continue after Paul Guillaume, an ambitious young art dealer, took an interest in his work and introduced him to sculptor Constantin Brâncuși. He was Constantin Brâncuși's disciple for one year.

Although a series of Modigliani's sculptures were exhibited in the Salon d'Automne of 1912, by 1914 he abandoned sculpting and focused solely on his painting, a move precipitated by the difficulty in acquiring sculptural materials due to the outbreak of war, and by Modigliani's physical debilitation.

Modigliani painted a series of portraits of contemporary artists and friends in Montparnasse: Chaim Soutine, Moise Kisling, Pablo Picasso, Diego Rivera, Marie "Marevna" Vorobyev-Stebeslka, Juan Gris, Max Jacob, Blaise Cendrars, and Jean Cocteau, all sat for stylized renditions.

At the outset of World War I, Modigliani tried to enlist in the army but was refused because of his poor health.

Known as Modì, which translates as 'cursed' (maudit), by many Parisians, but as Dedo to his family and friends, Modigliani was a handsome man, and attracted much female attention. Women came and went until Beatrice Hastings entered his life. She stayed with him for almost two years, was the subject for several of his portraits.

In 1916, Modigliani befriended the Polish poet and art dealer Leopold Zborowski and his wife Anna. Zborowski became Modigliani's primary art dealer and friend during the artist's final years, helping him financially, and also organizing his show in Paris in 1917.

The several dozen nudes Modigliani painted between 1916 and 1919 constitute many of his best-known works. This series of nudes was commissioned by Modigliani's dealer and friend Leopold Zborowski, who lent the artist use of his apartment, supplied models and painting materials, and paid him between fifteen and twenty francs each day for his work.

The paintings from this arrangement were thus different from his previous depictions of friends and lovers in that they were funded by Zborowski either for his own collection, as a favor to his friend, or with an eye to their "commercial potential", rather than originating from the artist's personal circle of acquaintances.

The Paris show of 1917 was Modigliani's only solo exhibition during his life, and is "notorious" in modern art history for its sensational public reception and the attendant issues of obscenity. The show was closed by police on its opening day, but continued thereafter, most likely after the removal of paintings from the gallery's street front window.

In the spring of 1917, the Russian sculptor Chana Orloff introduced him to a beautiful 19-year-old art student named Jeanne Hébuterne. From a conservative bourgeois background, Hébuterne was renounced by her devout Roman Catholic family for her liaison with the painter, whom they saw as little more than a debauched derelict. Despite her family's objections, soon they were living together, and although Hébuterne was the current love of his life, their public scenes became more renowned than Modigliani's individual drunken exhibitions.

After he and Hébuterne moved to Nice, she became pregnant, and on November 29, 1918, gave birth to a daughter whom they named Jeanne.

Although he continued to paint, Modigliani's health was deteriorating rapidly, and his alcohol-induced blackouts became more frequent. In 1920, after not hearing from him for several days, his downstairs neighbor checked on the family and found Modigliani in bed delirious and holding onto Hébuterne, who was nearly nine months pregnant. They summoned a doctor, but little could be done because Modigliani was in the final stage of his disease, dying of tubercular meningitis.

Modigliani died on January 24, 1920. There was an enormous funeral, attended by many from the artistic communities in Montmartre and Montparnasse.

Paintings

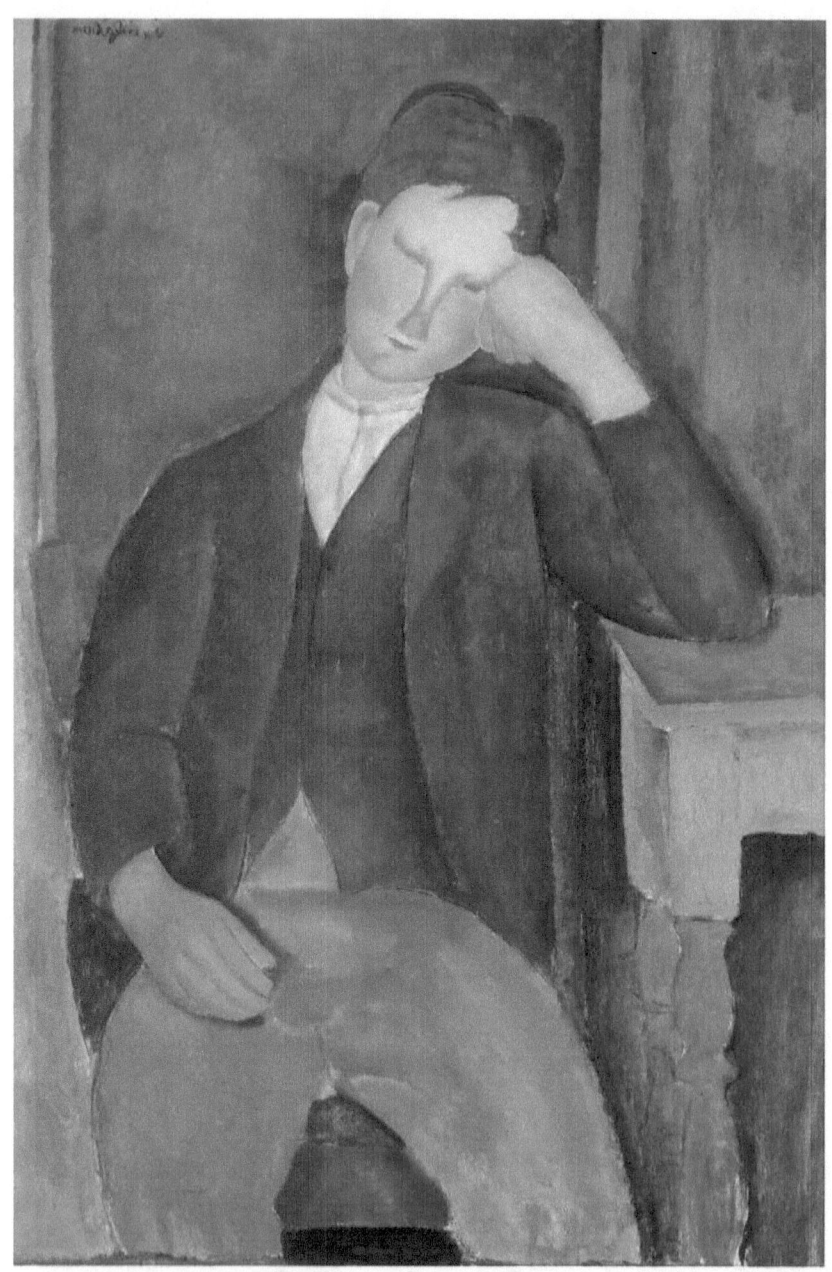

The Young Apprentice
1918 – 1919, oil on canvas, Musée de l'Orangerie, Paris

Firmly installed in the space of the table, the figure gives an impression of stability. The lines of the rear door, chair and table show the flexible forms the model's body. All muscles are released with the exception of those of the left arm with elbow rests on the table for the hand supports the head. This is a pose that is found in models of Cézanne-smokers or drinkers seated - and Modigliani admired. Own attitude at rest, eyes half-closed or conducive to meditation, it gives the opportunity to camp Modigliani individuality laborious. If the hand supports the head wife indeed the complexion of the face, which rests on the thigh of his weight, is a color as incandescent burned by exercise.

The range of colors is usual that usually used by the artist - blue off, scorched earth, beige khaki pants. Only the color of the hand of a dazzling pink carries with it the fate of the doomed teenager physical effort.

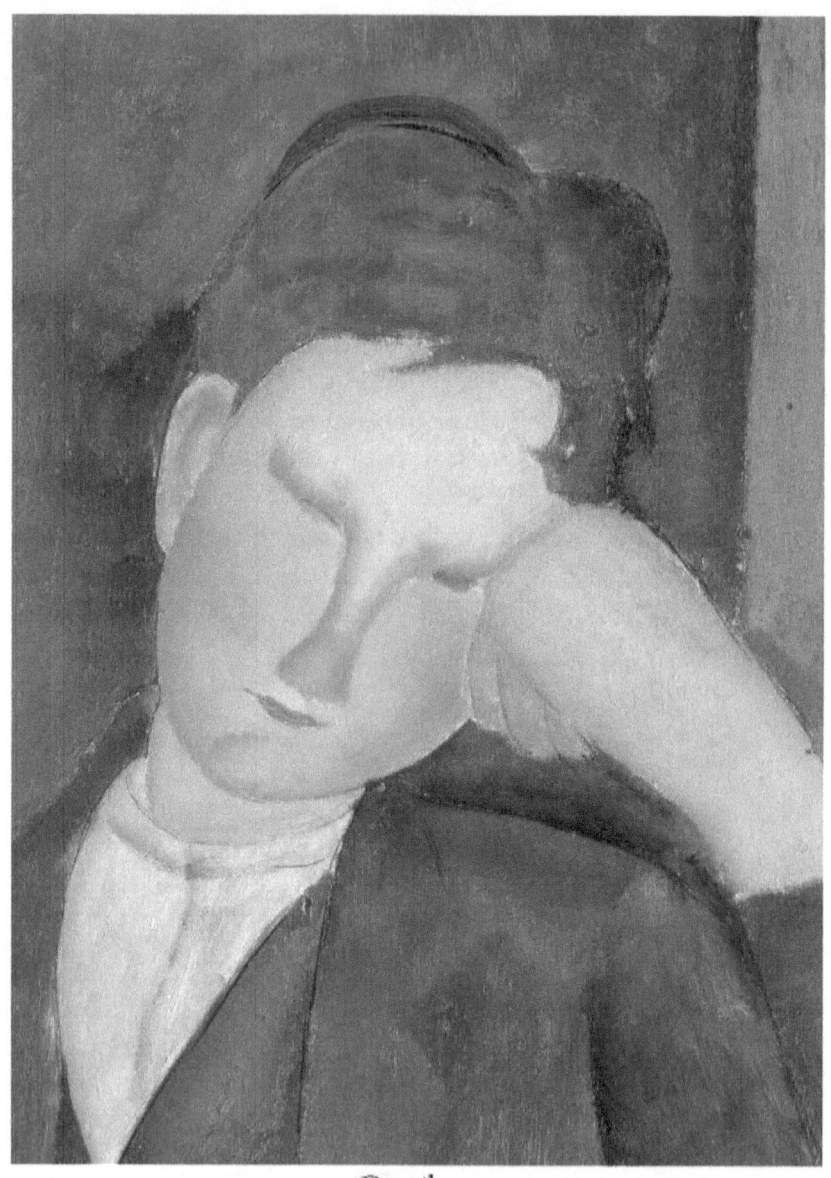

Detail

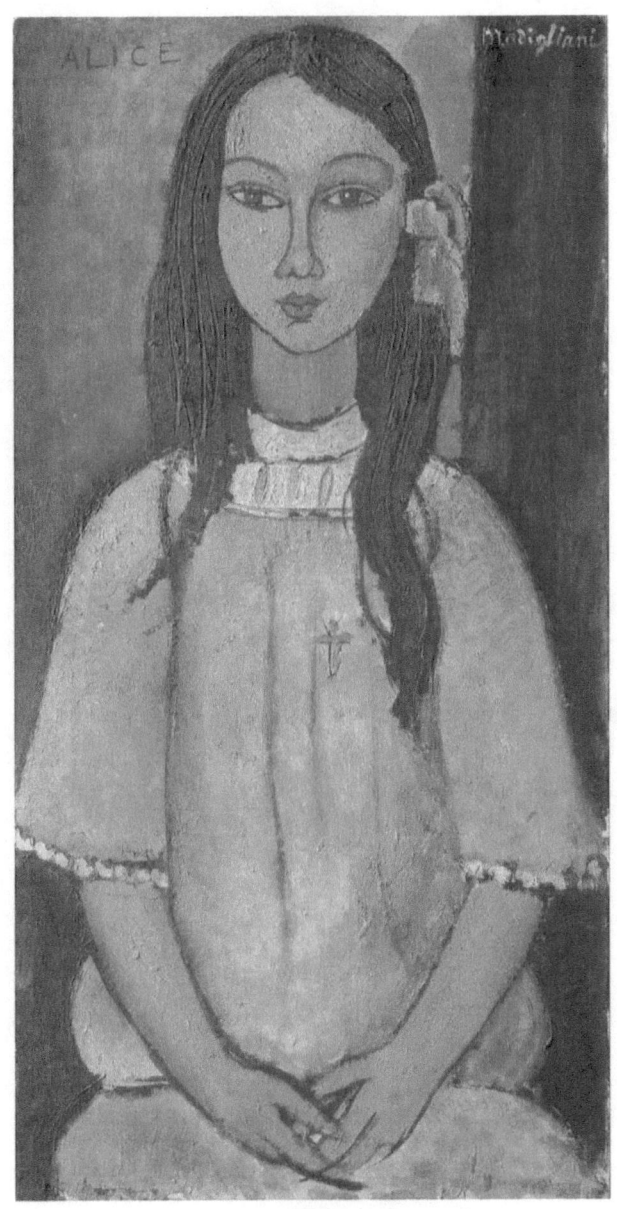

Alice
1918, Oil on Canvas

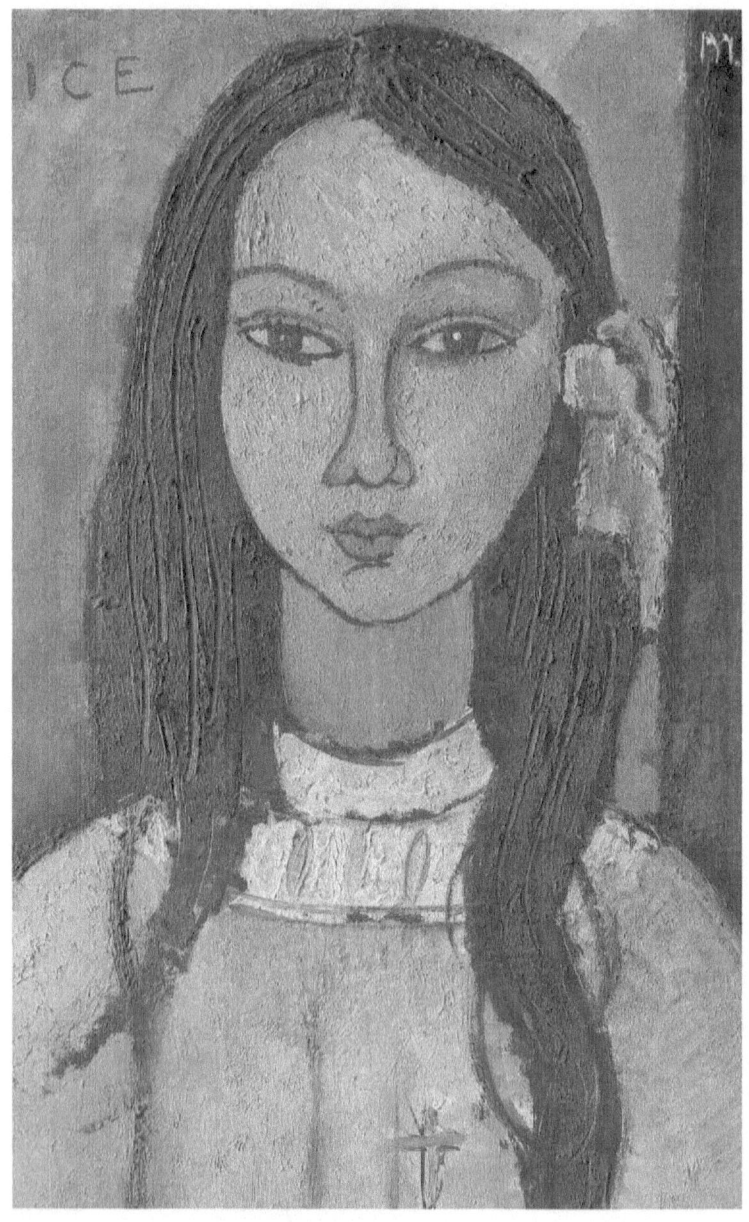

Detail

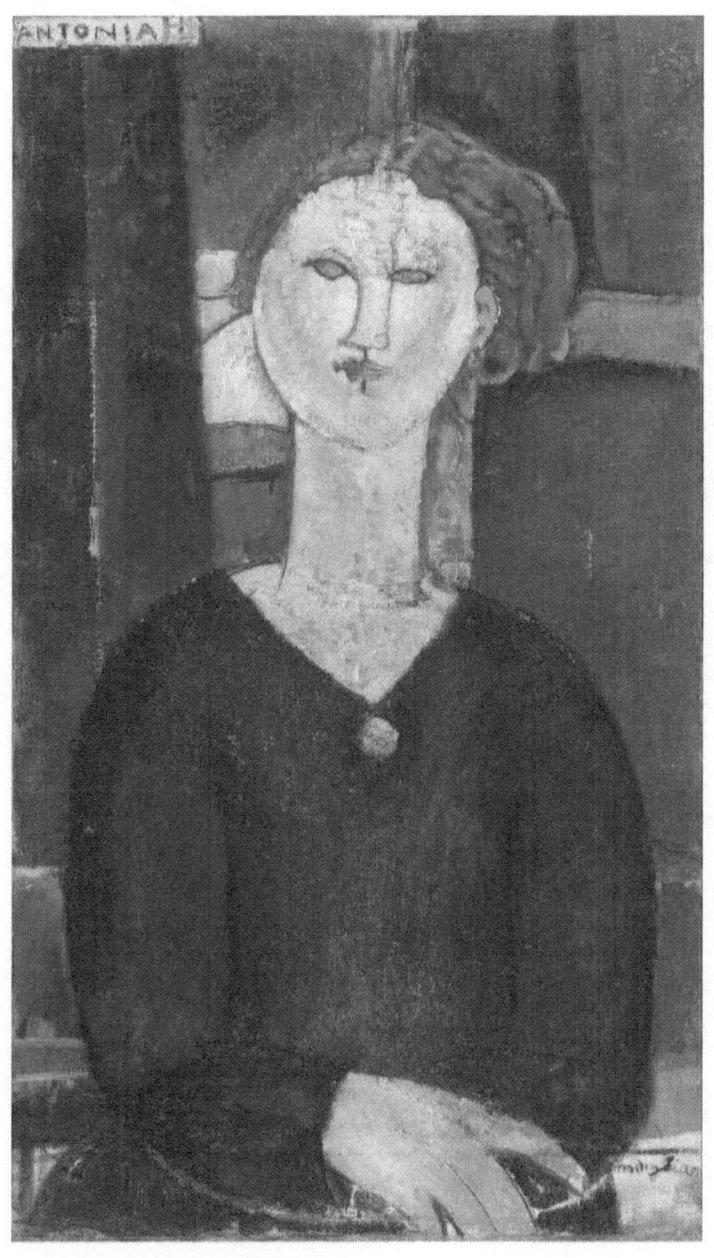

Antonia
1915, Oil on Canvas

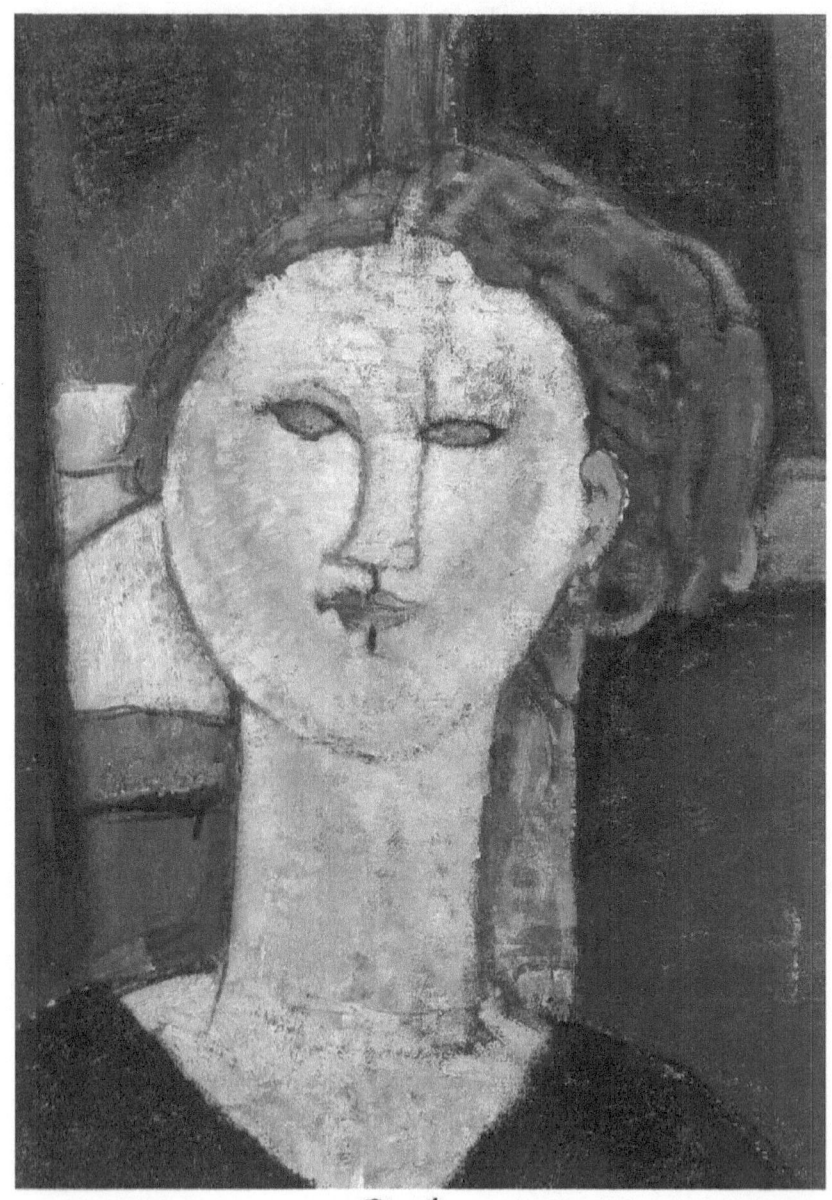

Detail

MODIGLIANI

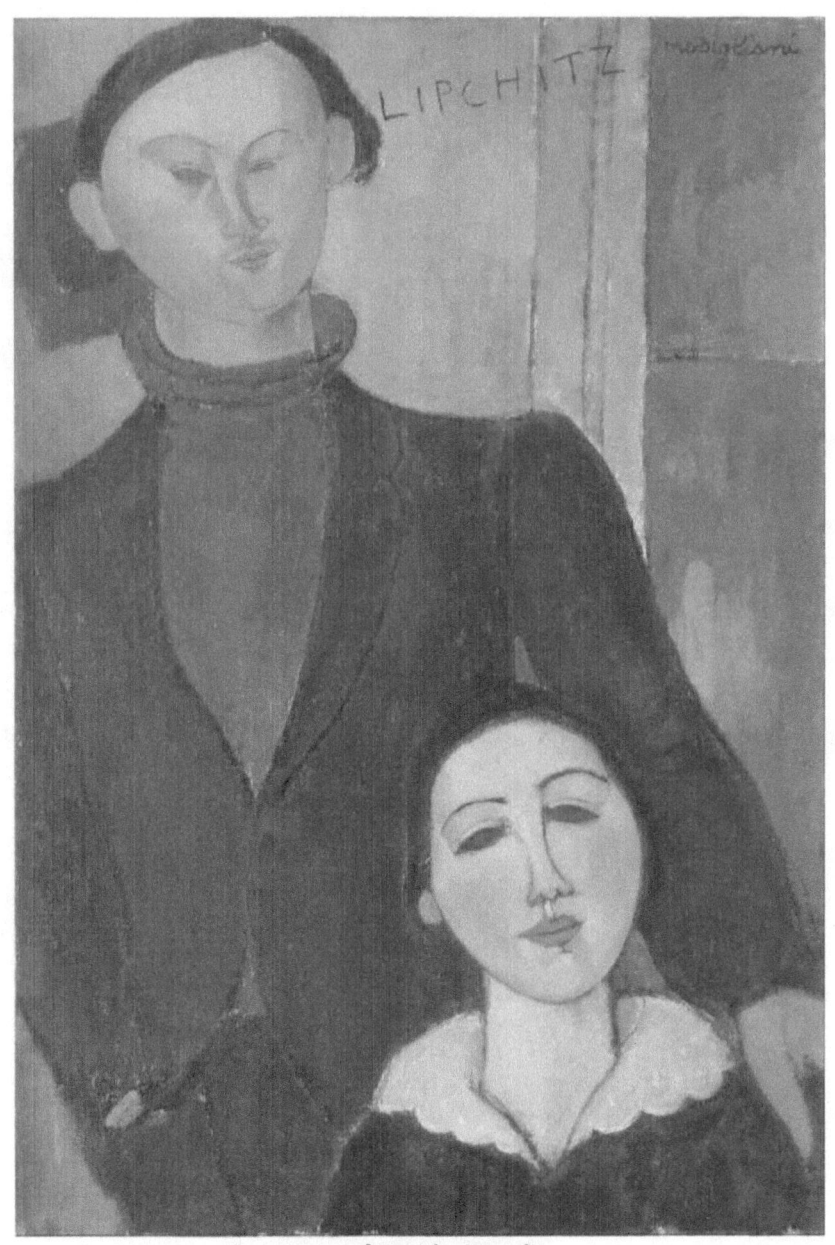

Jacques and Berthe Lipchitz
1916, Oil on Canvas

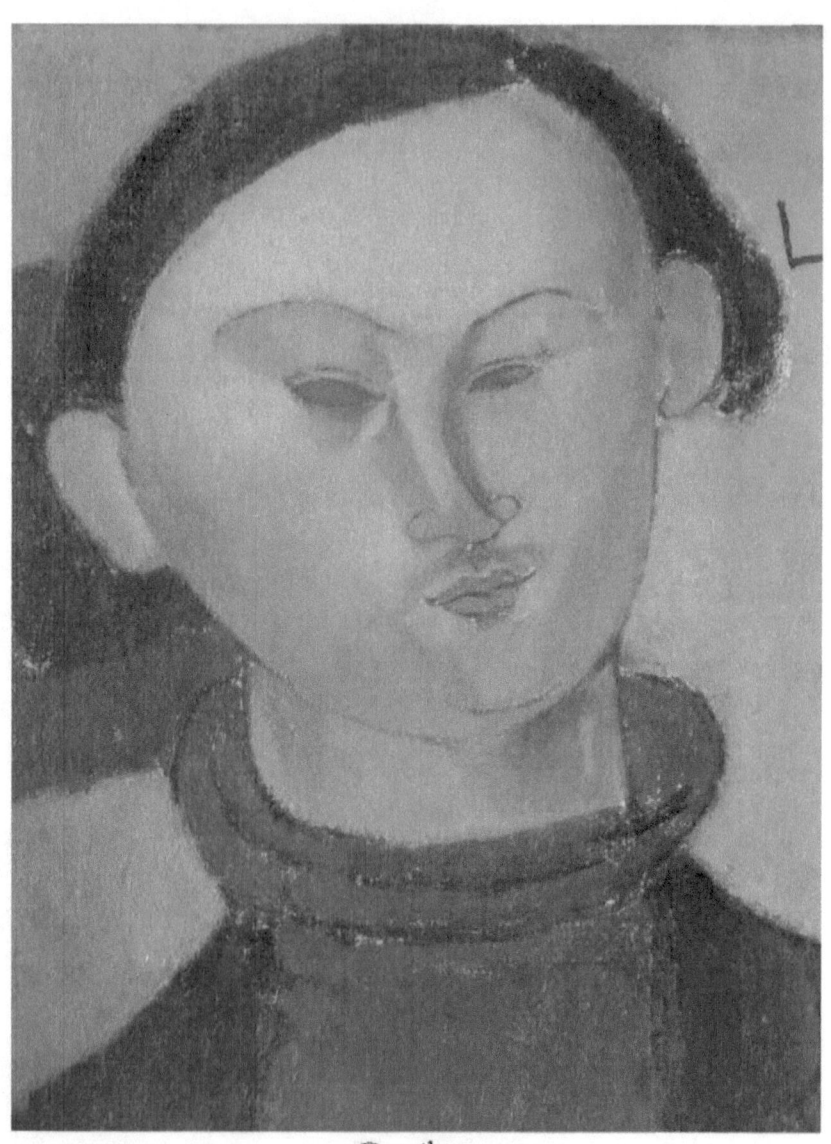

Detail

MODIGLIANI

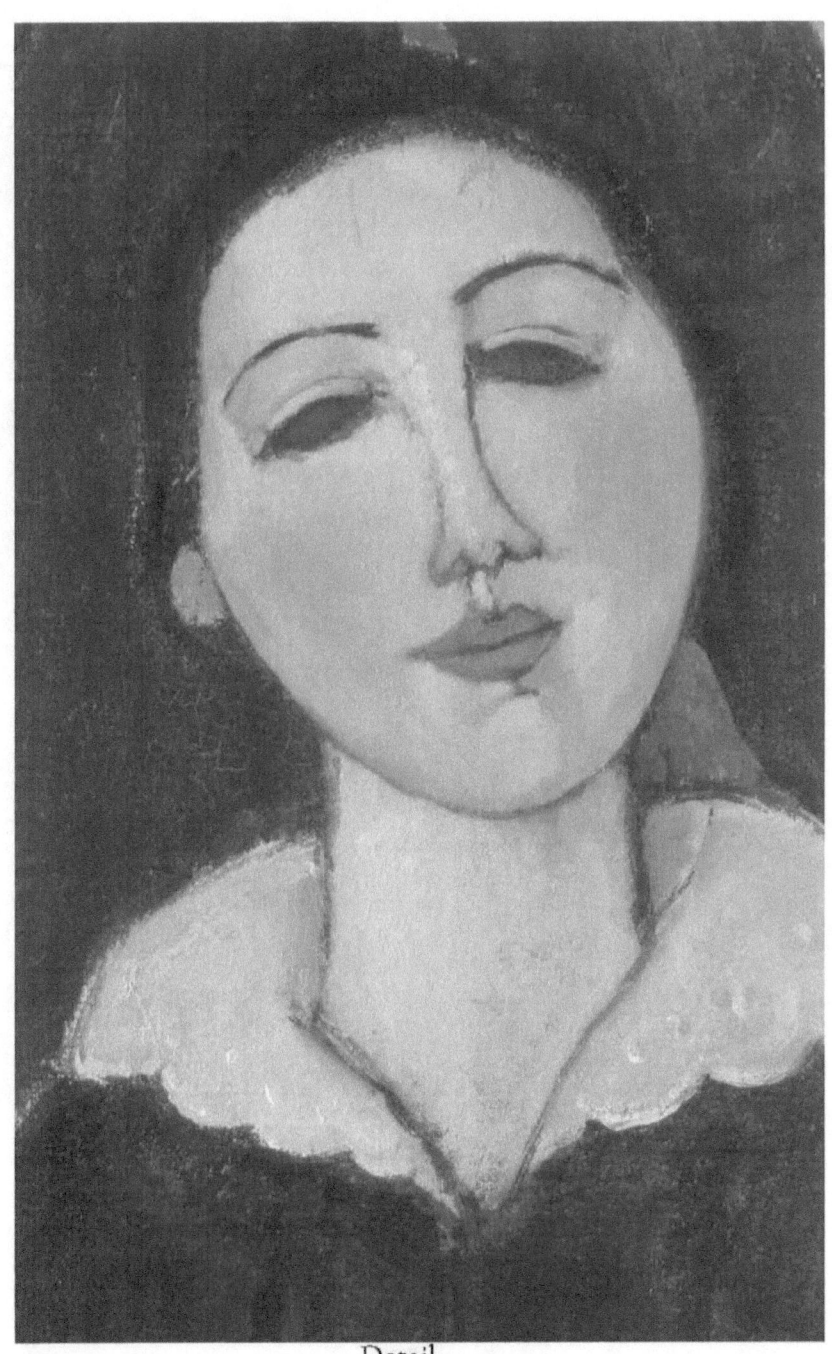

Detail

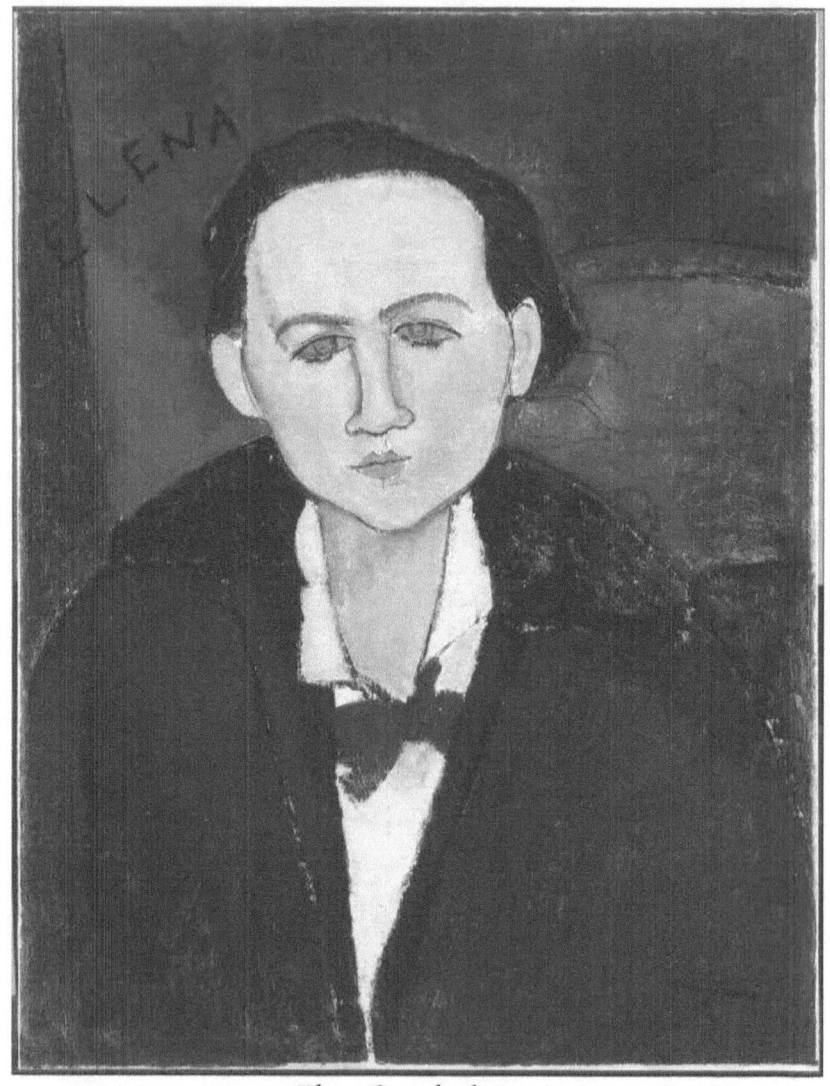

Elena Povolozky
1917, Oil on canvas, 25 ½ x 19 1/8 in, Public Collection
The present work, painted in Paris in 1917 when Modigliani was ending his affair with Beatrice Hastings and beginning a relationship with Jeanne Hebertune, represents the Polish woman,

MODIGLIANI

Elena Povlovzky, believed to be a member of the Montmartre intellectual circle. Leopold Zborowski, the Polish entrepreneur who became Modigliani's dealer, may have introduced Povlozky to the artist. The present painting and its subject have been compared to Picasso's celebrated portrayal of Gertrude Stein: both sitters share a forthright masculine demeanor.

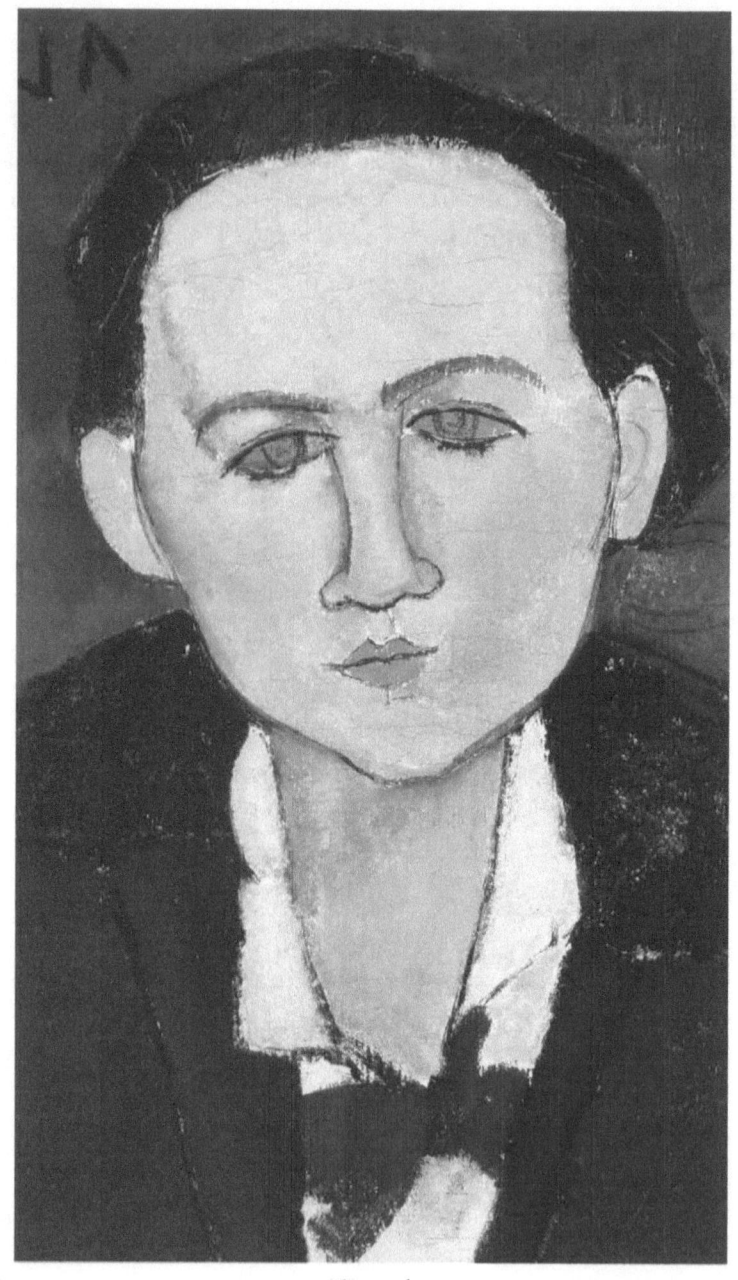

Detail

MODIGLIANI

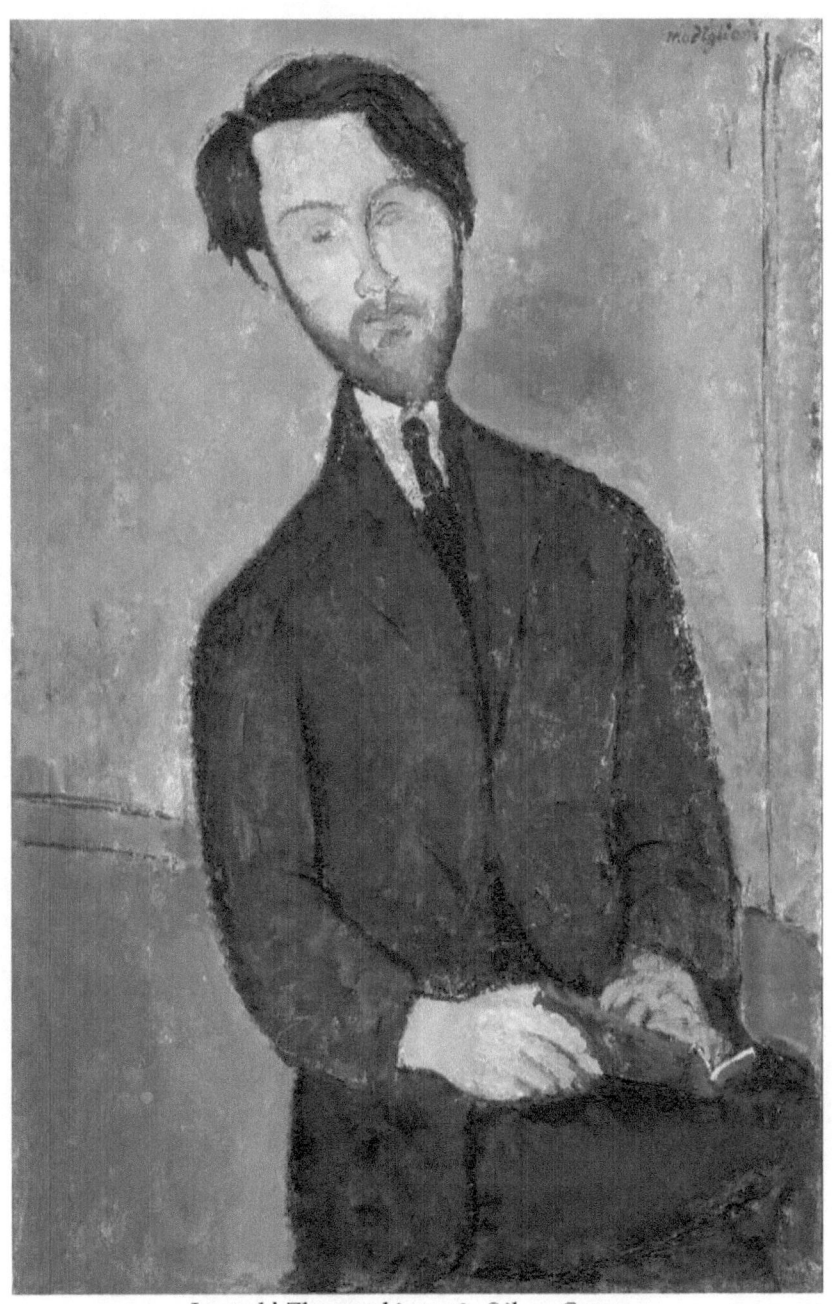

Leopold Zborowski, 1918, Oil on Canvas

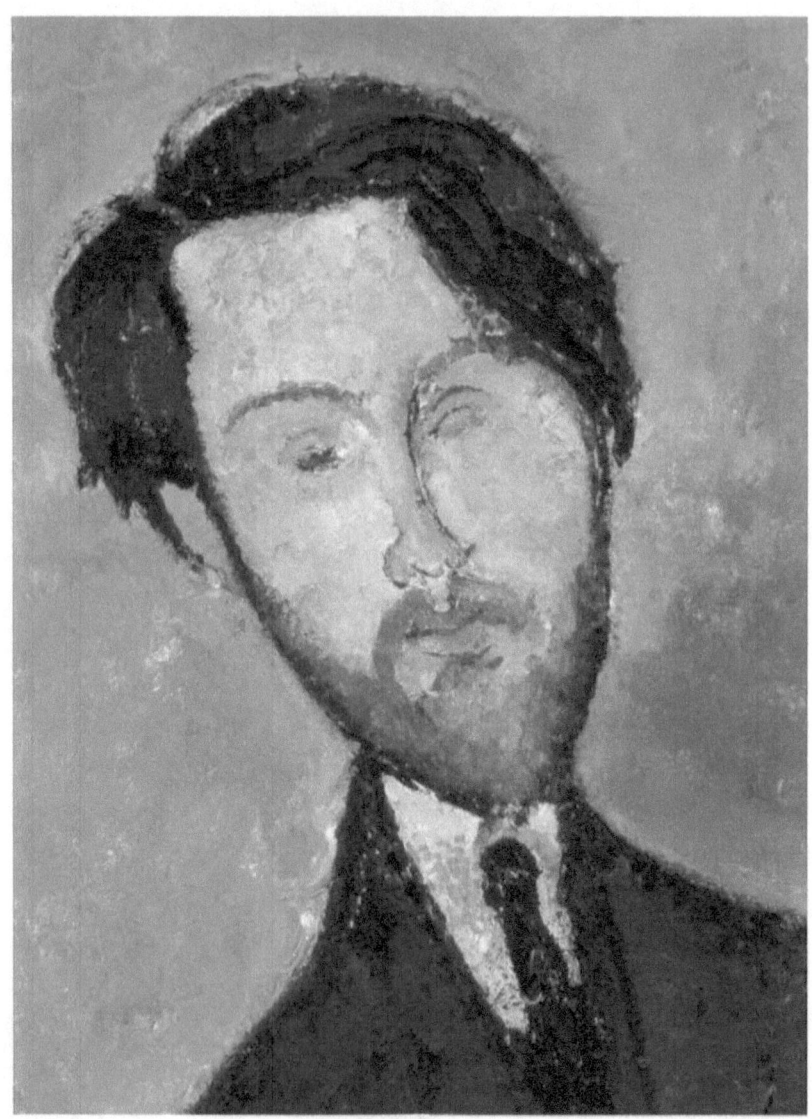

Detail

MODIGLIANI

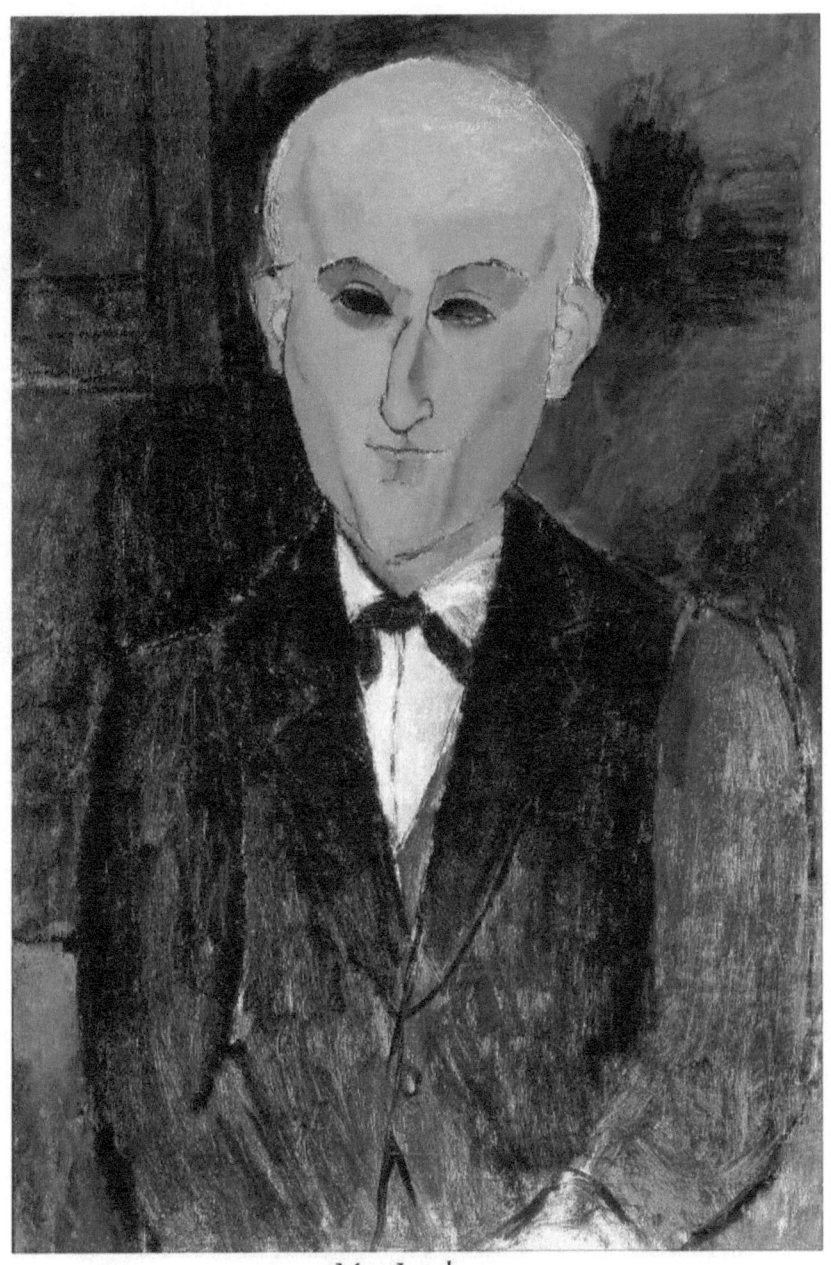

Max Jacob
1921, Oil on Canvas

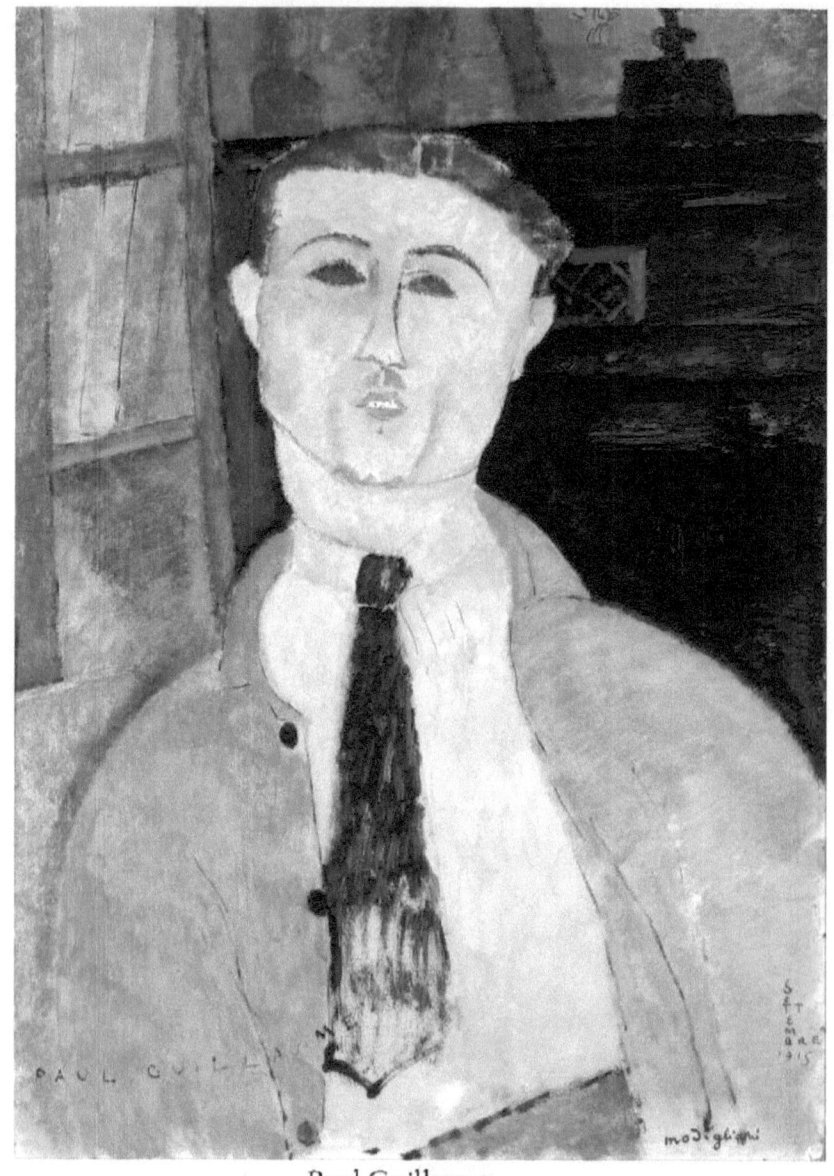

Paul Guillaume
1915, Oil on Canvas

MODIGLIANI

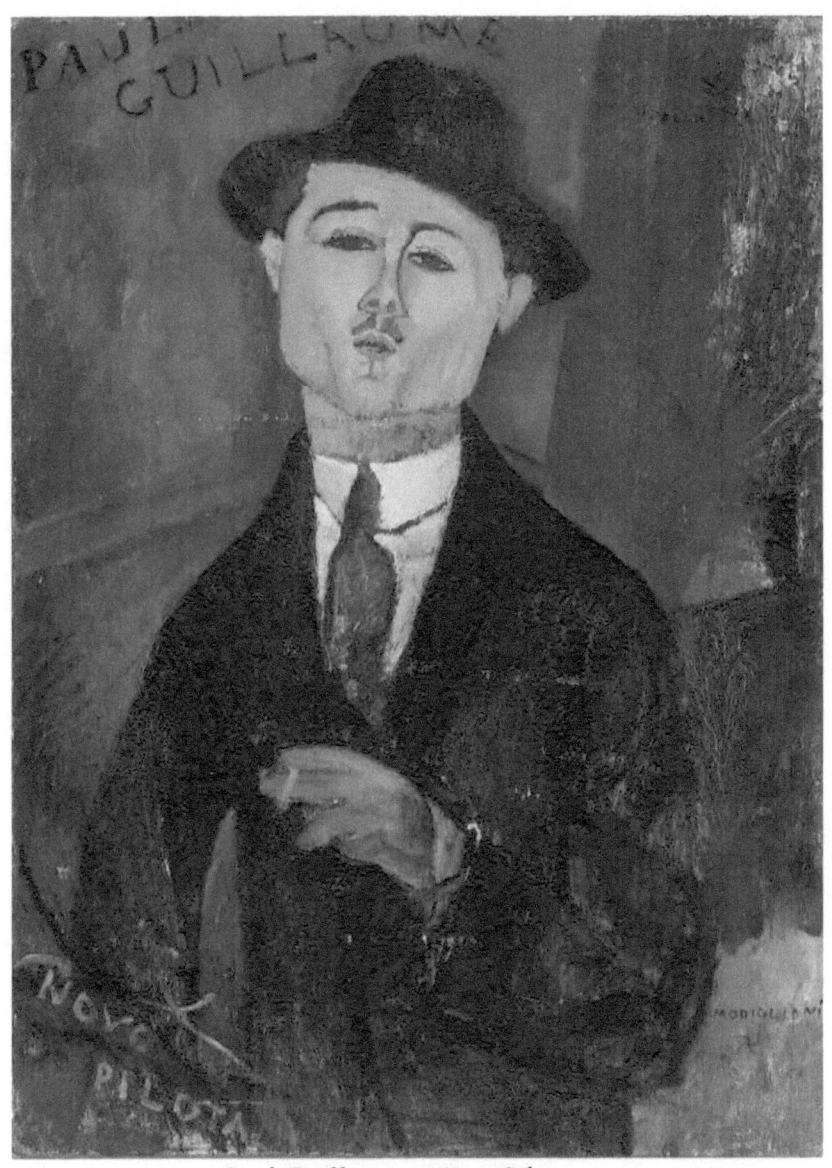

Paul Guillaume, Novo Pilota
1915, oil on cardboard mounted on plywood floored against,
Musée de l'Orangerie, Paris

In 1915, Modigliani, then unknown, a portrait of a young well-dressed man, who fixed a slight casually Paul Guillaume, whose name appears in full in the upper left corner, appears here in its character young art dealer. Dressed in a black suit which contrasts with the white shirt accented with deep blue tie, he kept his hat and even his gloves into the cigarette he carelessly left hand adds a touch of familiarity the laying of a dandy. The bottom barely sketched reflects the counting of Modigliani's studio in Montmartre. The inscription "Novo Pilota" at the bottom of the table refers to the boldness of the model, which means, like a race car driver, take the reins of its destiny, and much of the art modern, with a mixture of recklessness and risk assumed. In fact, from 1914 to early 1916, Paul Guillaume is the sole buyer of Modigliani.

MODIGLIANI

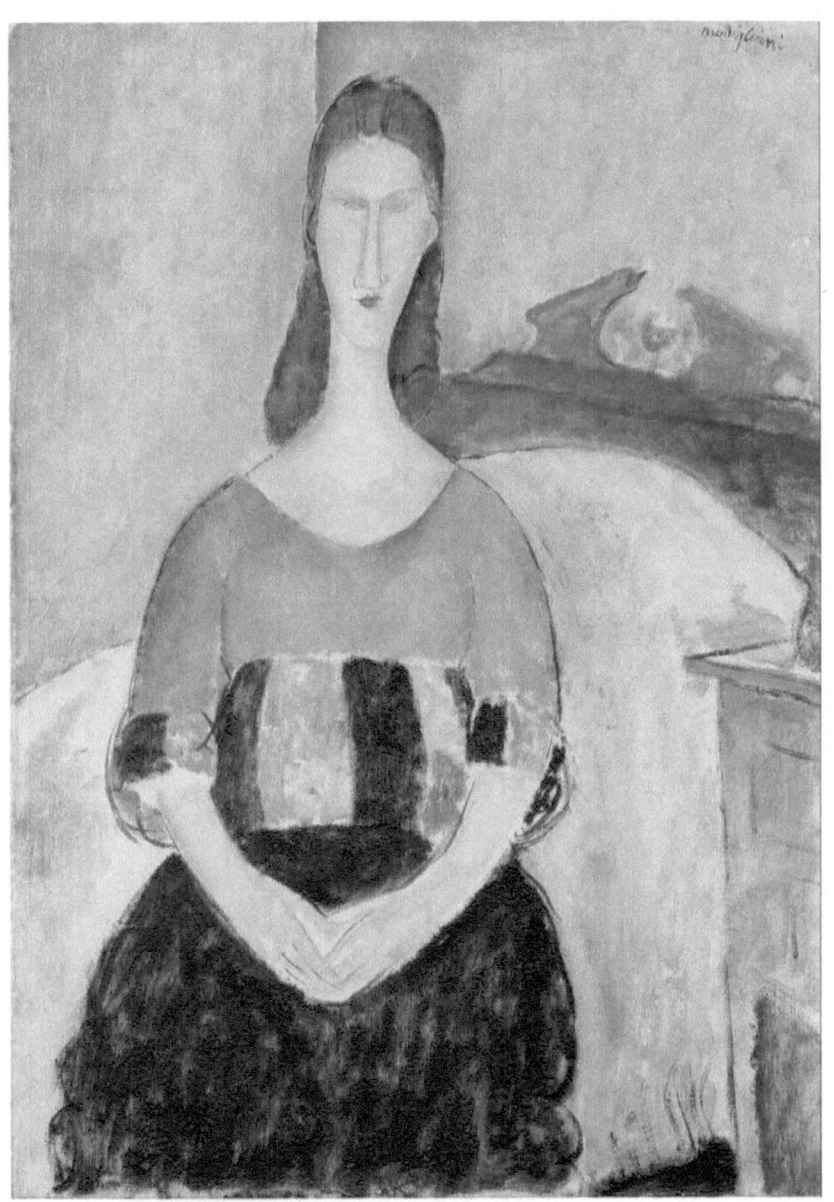

Portrait of Jeanne Hebuterne, Seated
1918, Oil on Canvas

Jessica Findley

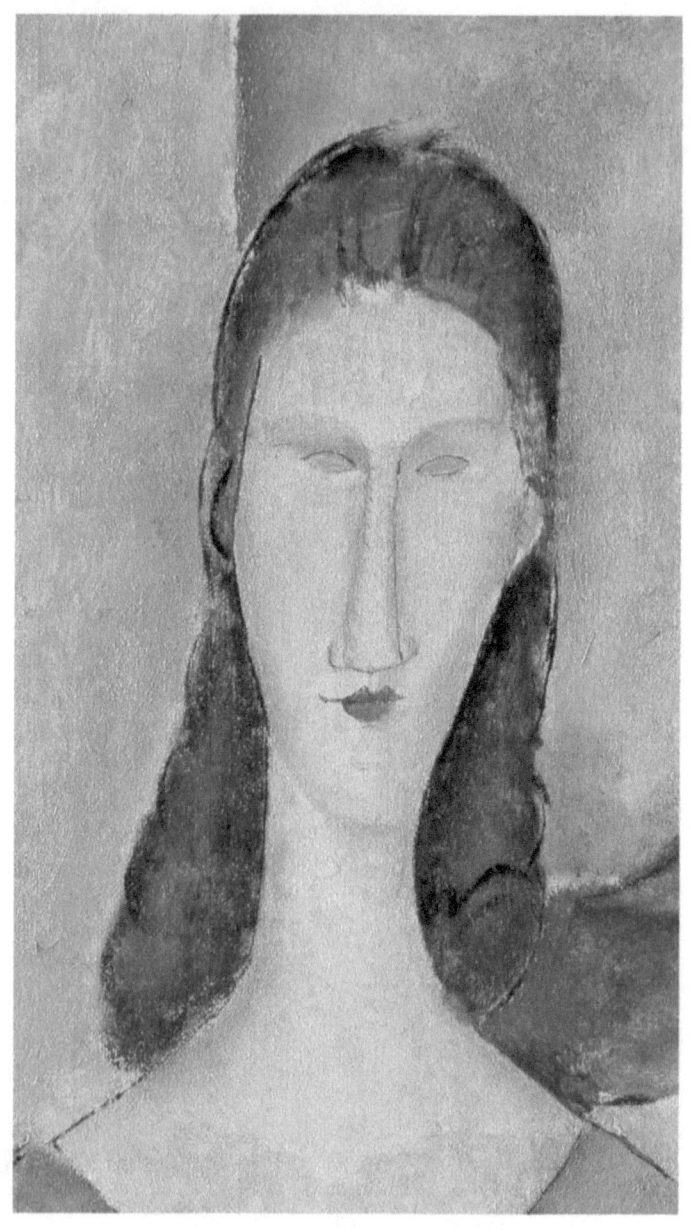

Detail

MODIGLIANI

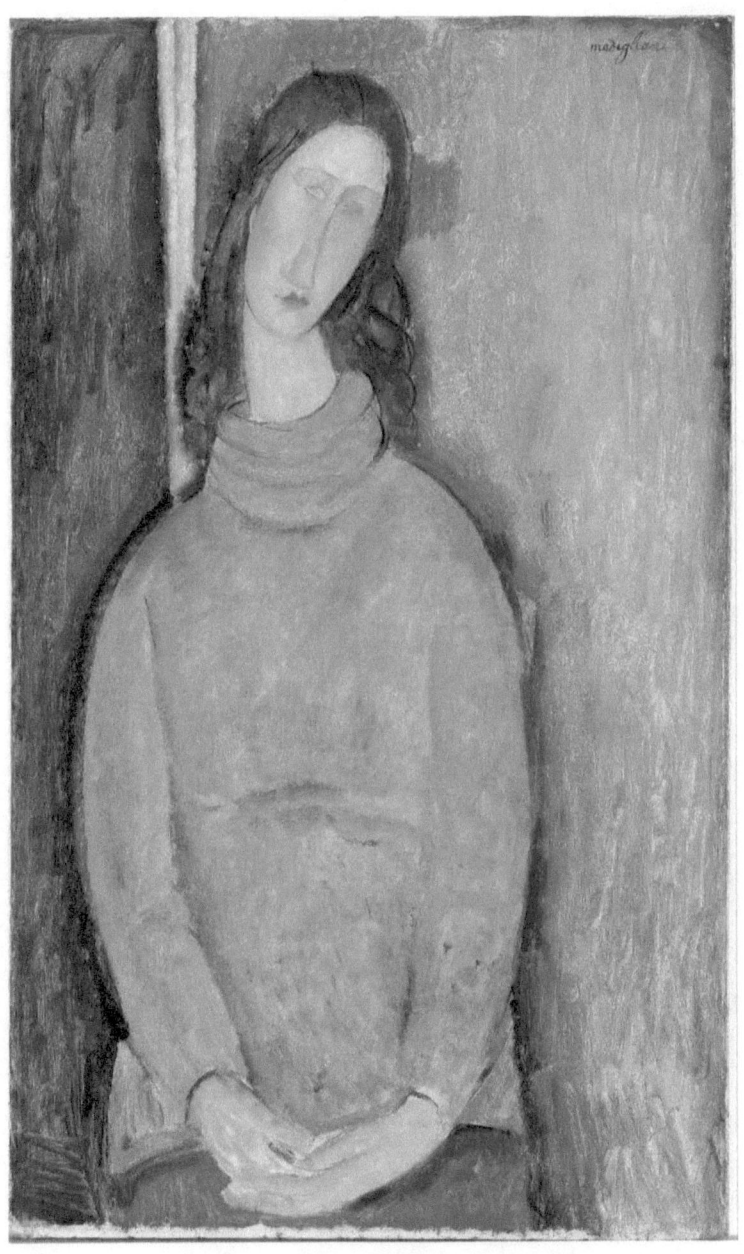

Portrait of Jeanne Hébuterne
1919, Oil on Canvas

Jessica Findley

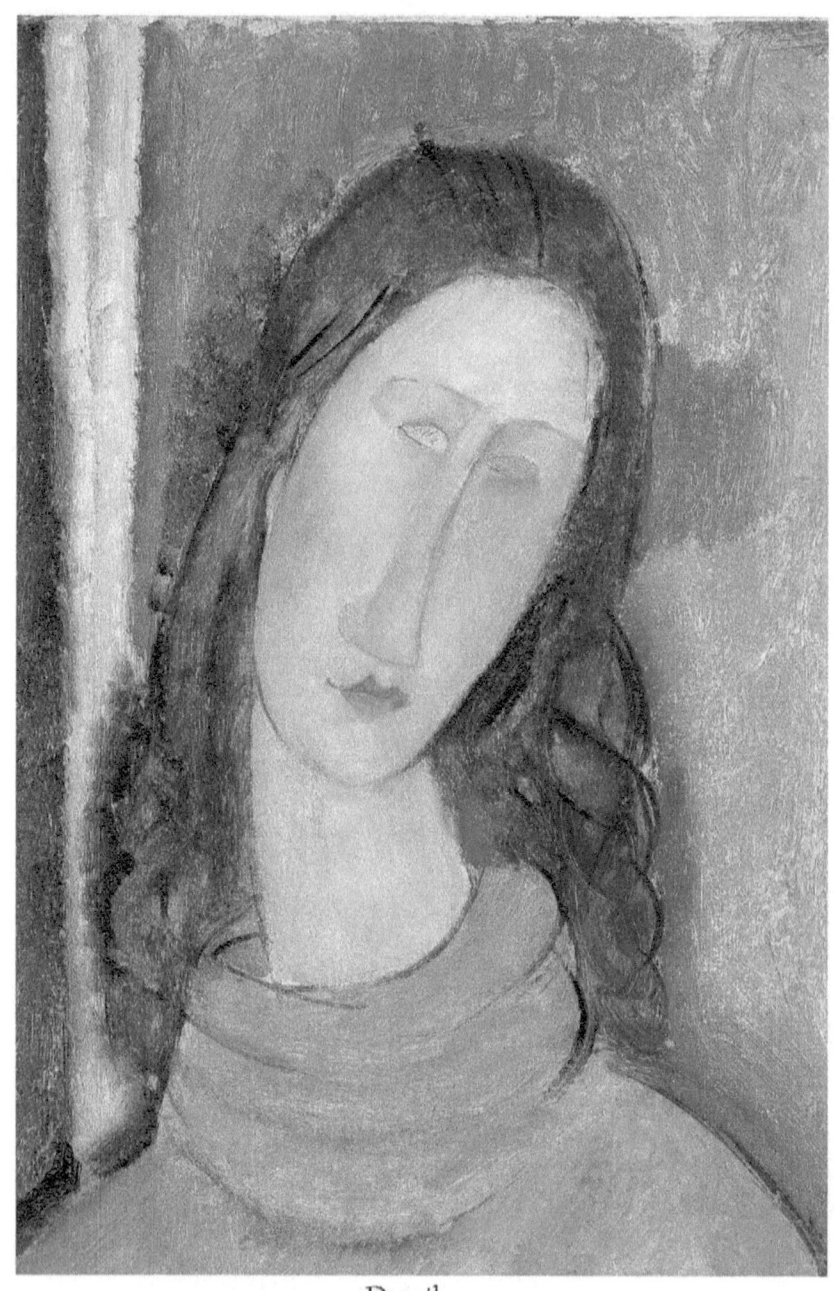

Detail

MODIGLIANI

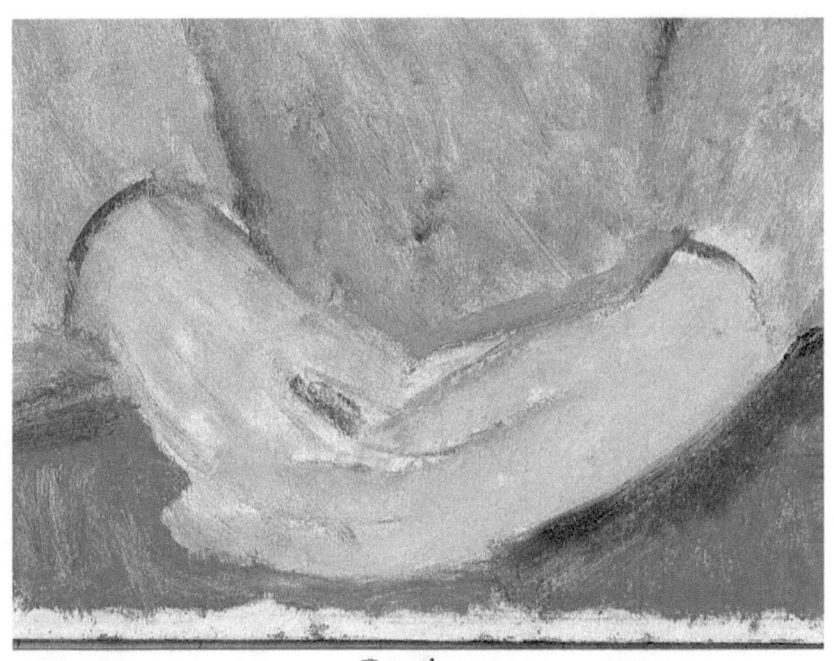

Detail

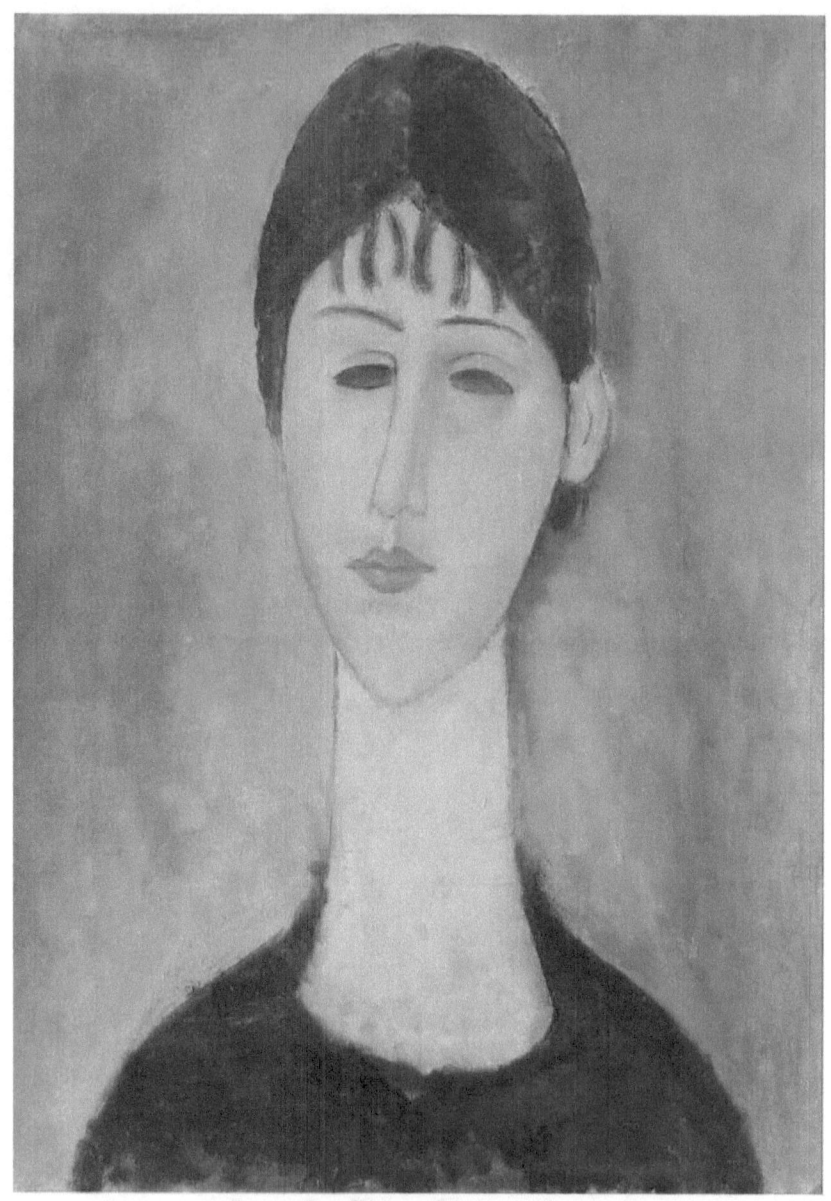

Portrait of Mme Zborowska
1918, Oil on Canvas

MODIGLIANI

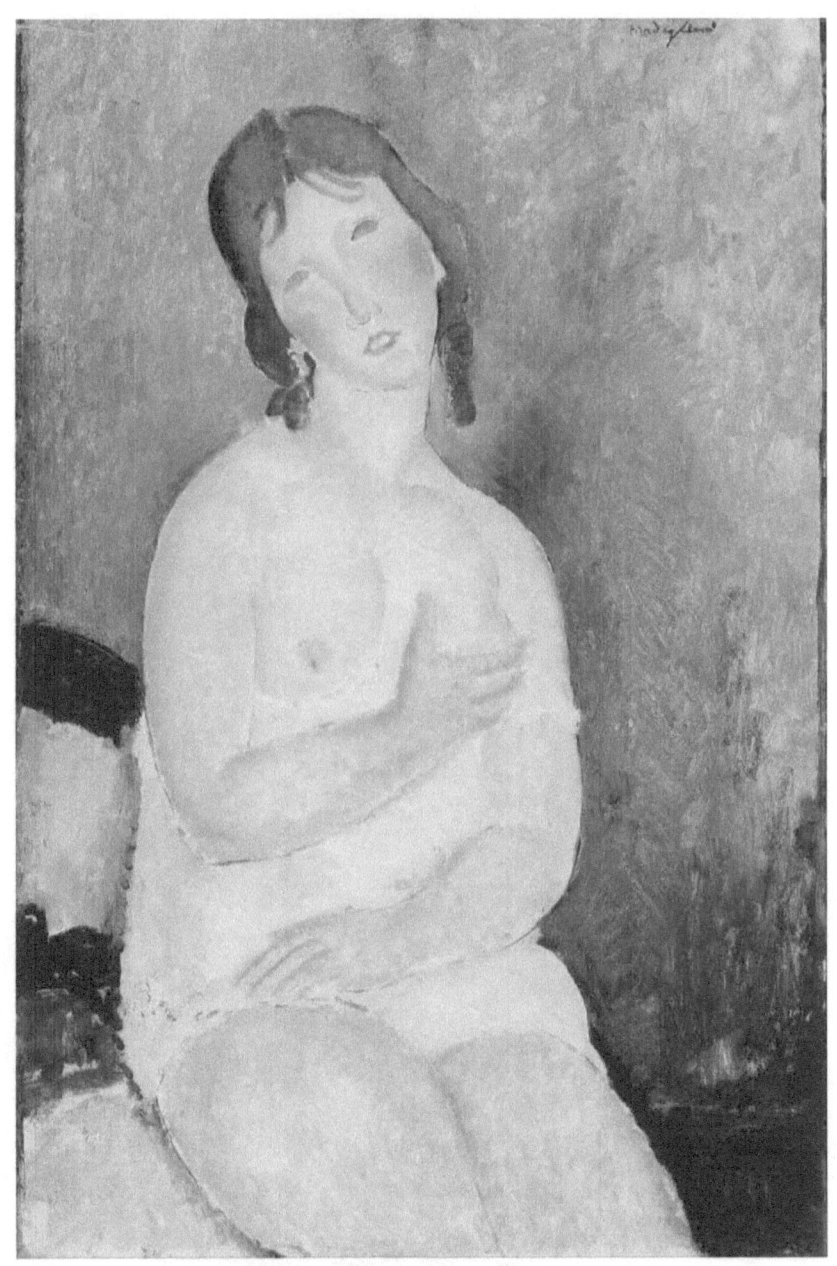

Young Woman in a Shirt
1918, Oil on Canvas

Jessica Findley

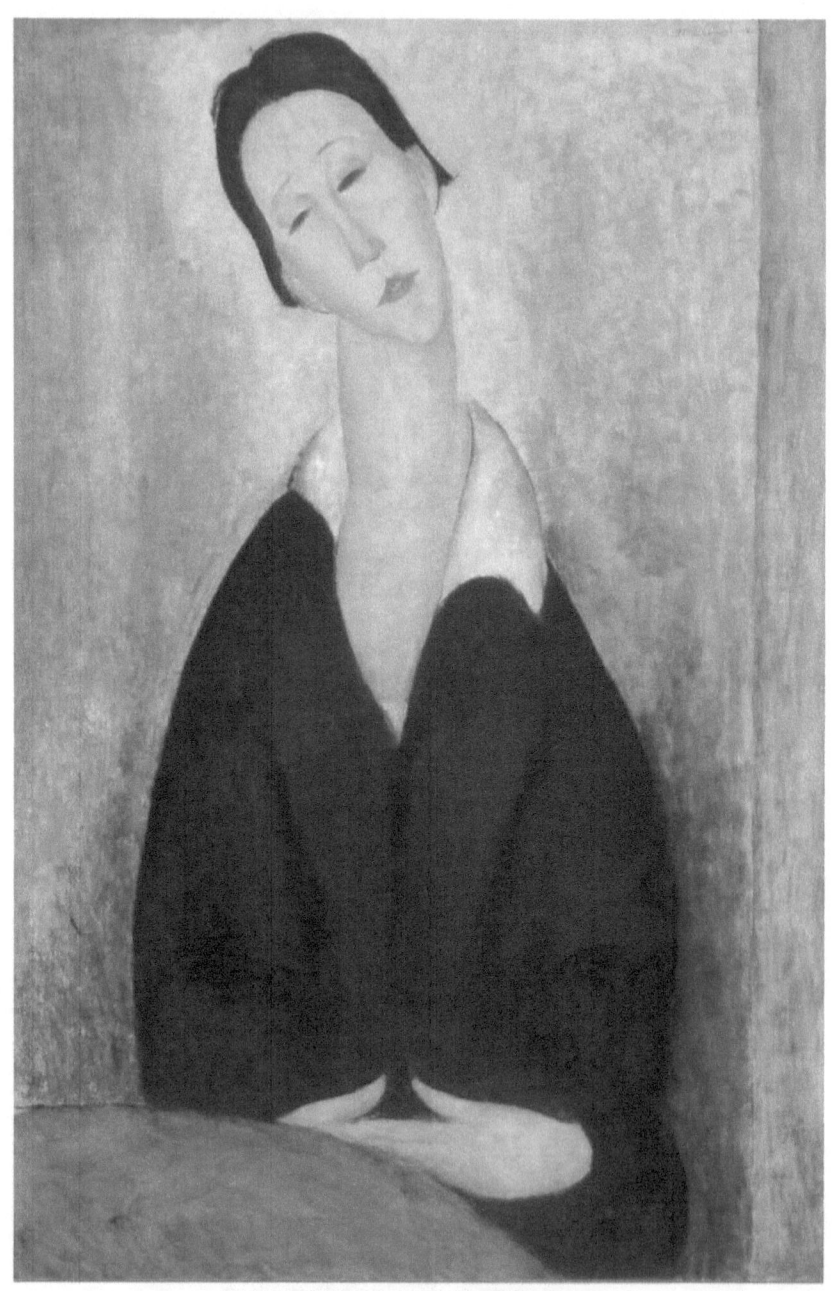

Portrait of a Polish Woman
1919, Oil on canvas, 100.3 x 64.8 cm, Philadelphia Museum

MODIGLIANI

Portrait of a Polish Woman exemplifies Amedeo Modigliani's favorite choice of subject: the single figure, most often female, filling the frame, isolated from incidental detail, and directly confronting the artist and viewer. The unidentified sitter here is most likely Hanka Zborowska, the aristocratic Polish wife of Modigliani's most devoted dealer, Leopold Zborowski. Zborowska, along with her close friend Luina Czechowska, another Polish woman who might also be the subject of this portrait, both posed frequently for Modigliani in the last years of his life. The use of friends for models, a practice that began out of financial necessity, resulted in a number of penetrating encounters for Modigliani, challenging him to achieve a balance between strong individual character and the emphatic imprint of his style. In this portrait, Modigliani's propensity for fluid linearity, geometric simplification, and elongation and displacement of body parts - not unexpected for an artist sometimes described as an inheritor of the Italian Mannerist tradition - underscores the elegance and sophistication of his sitter.

Jessica Findley

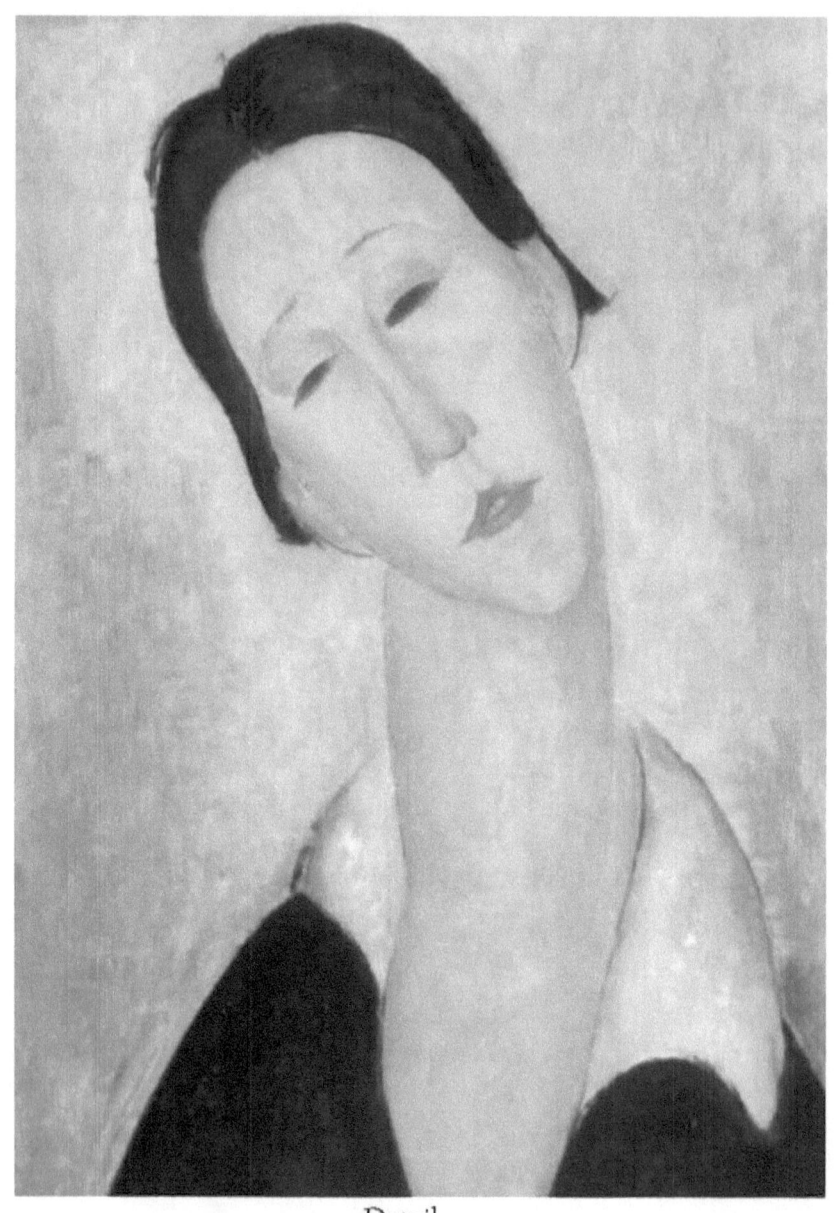

Detail

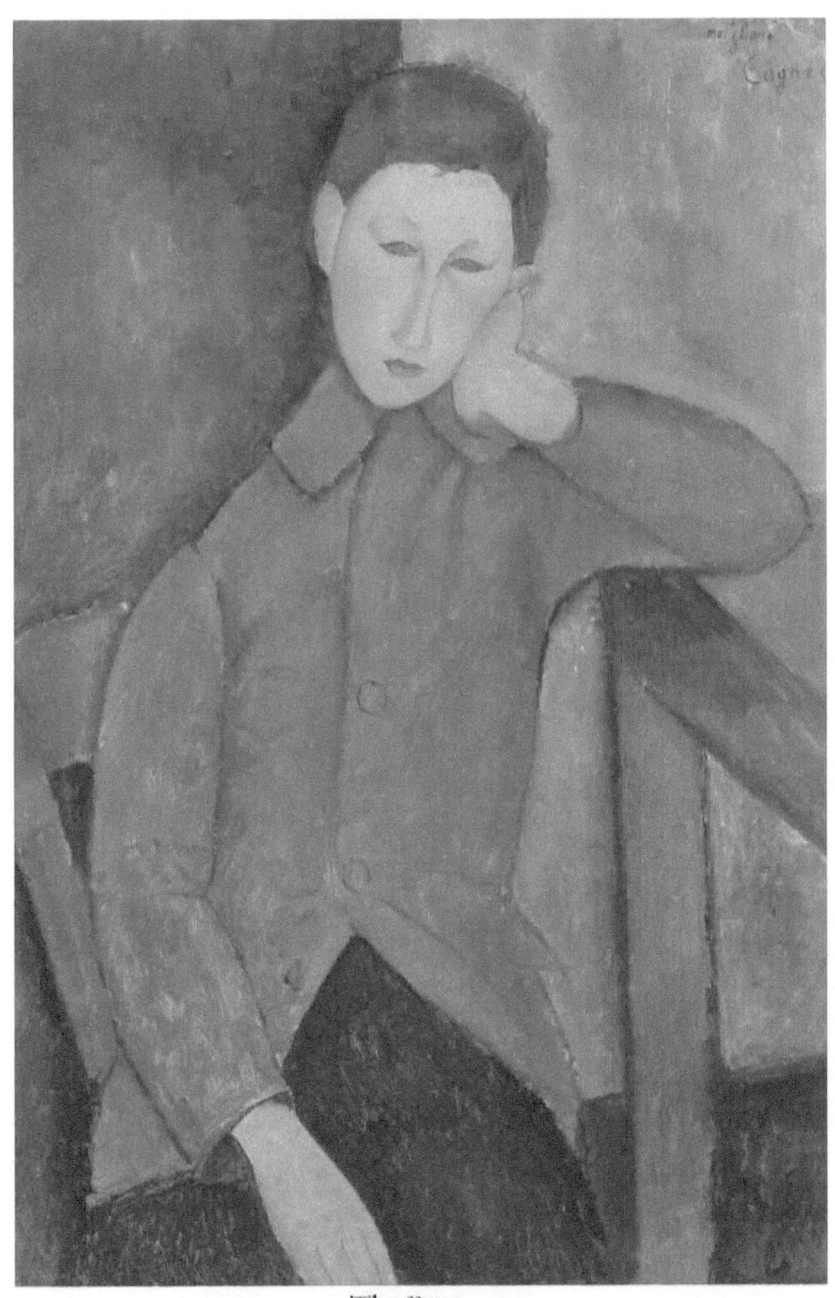

The Boy
1919, Oil on Canvas

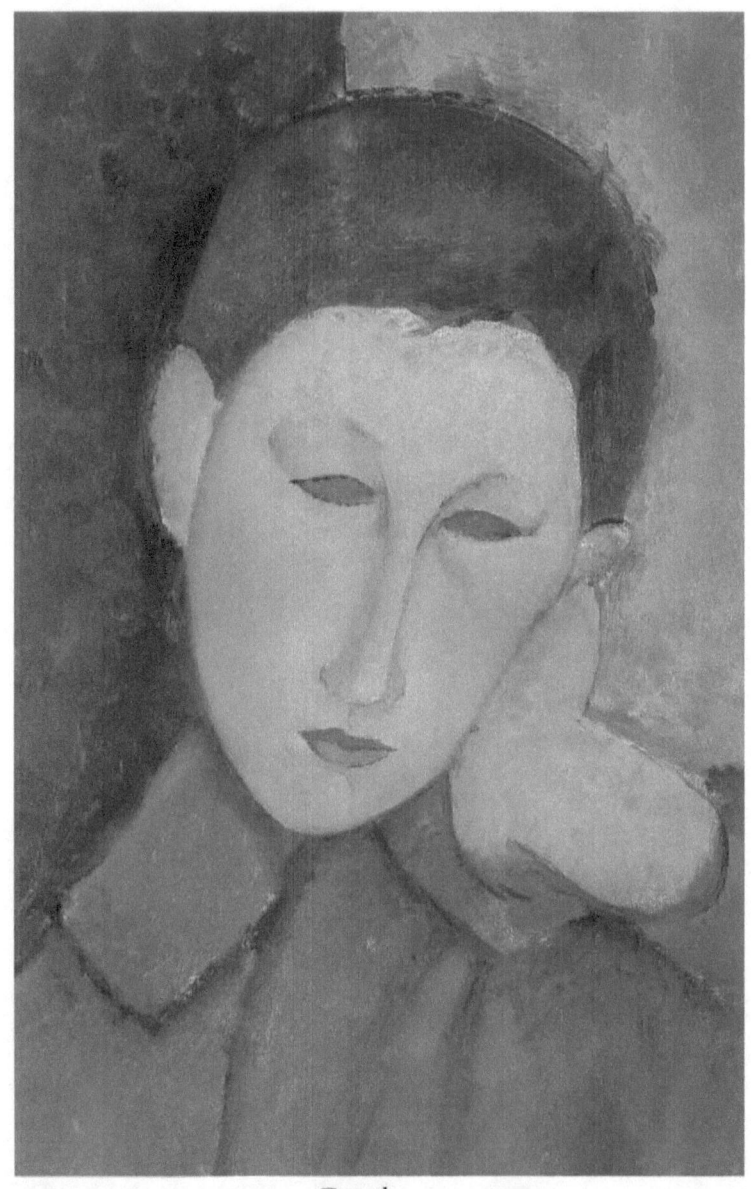

Detail

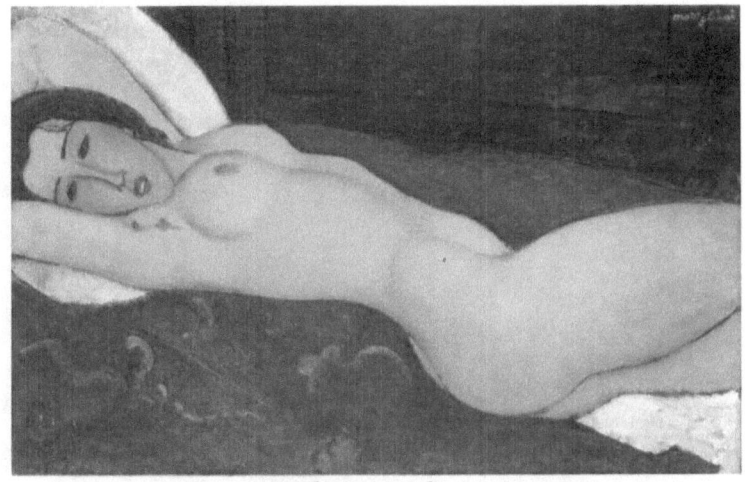

Reclining Nude
1917, Oil on canvas, 60.6 x 92.7 cm, The Metropolitan
Museum of Art

Modigliani's celebrated series of nudes continues the tradition of depictions of Venuses from the Renaissance to the nineteenth century but with one significant difference: the eroticism of the earlier figures is always couched within a mythological or anecdotal context, whereas Modigliani does away with this pretext. Consequently, his women appear unabashedly frank and provocative.

The artist is best known for the works that he created in Paris between 1915 and 1919 — portraits, in which a few telling details achieve a striking likeness, and nudes. Modigliani began his great series of reclining women in 1916. The two dozen or so figures — never his mistresses or friends but always professional models — lie on a dark bed cover that accentuates the glow of their skin; they are seen close-up and usually from above. Their stylized bodies span the entire width of the canvas, and their hands and feet often remain outside the picture's frame.

Jessica Findley

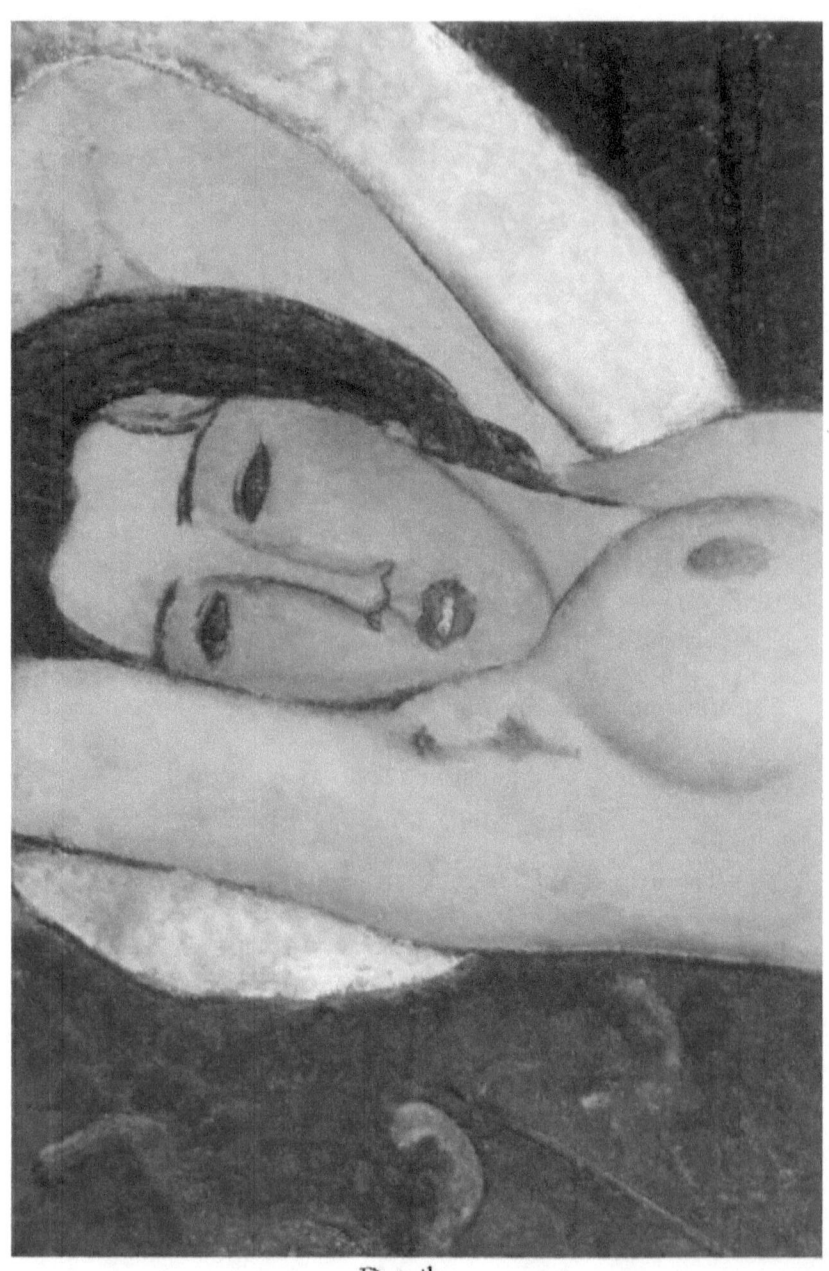

Detail

MODIGLIANI

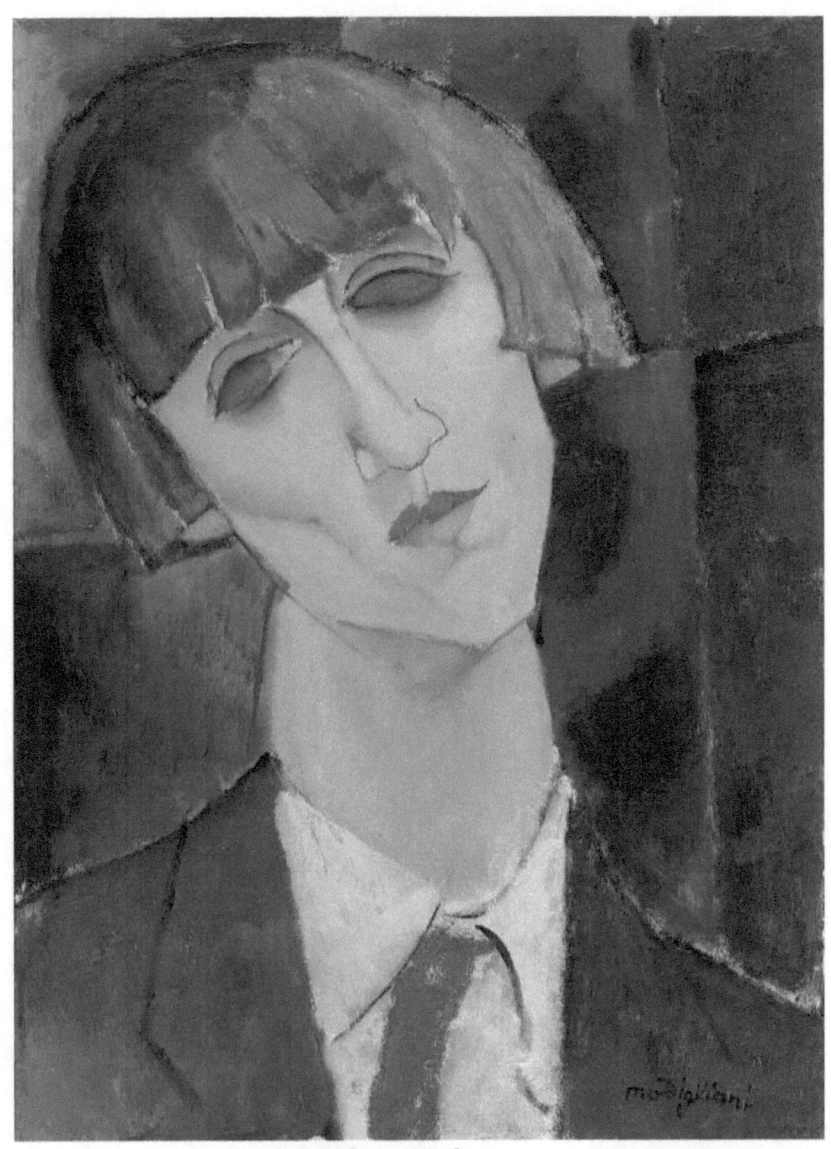

Madame Kisling
1917, Oil on Canvas

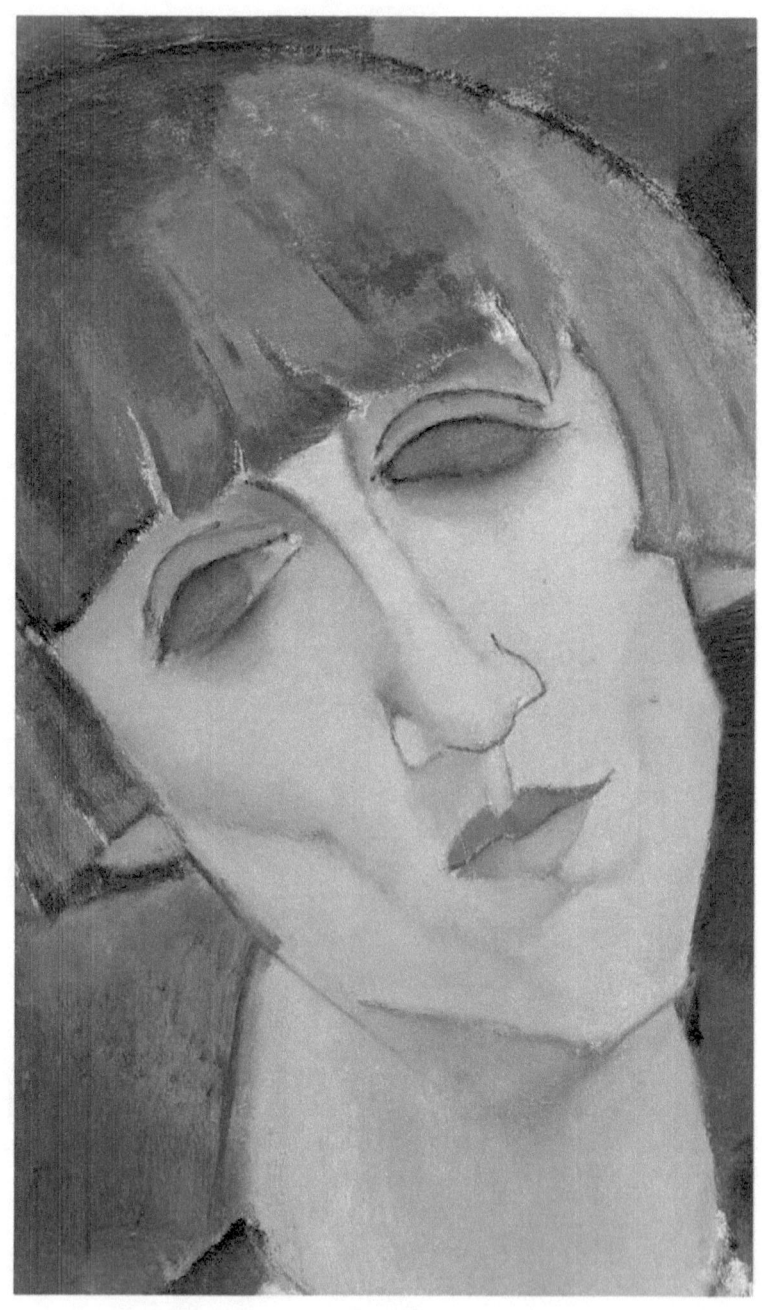

Detail

MODIGLIANI

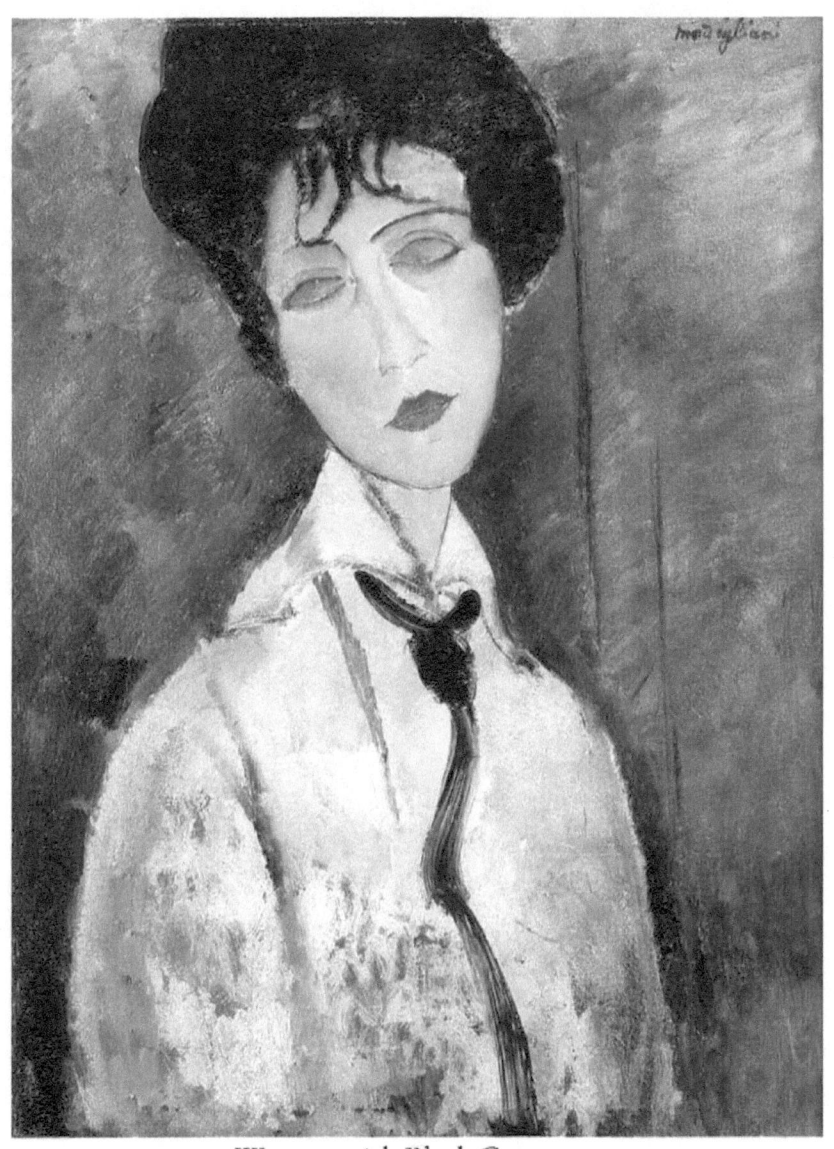

Woman with Black Cravat
Oil on Canvas

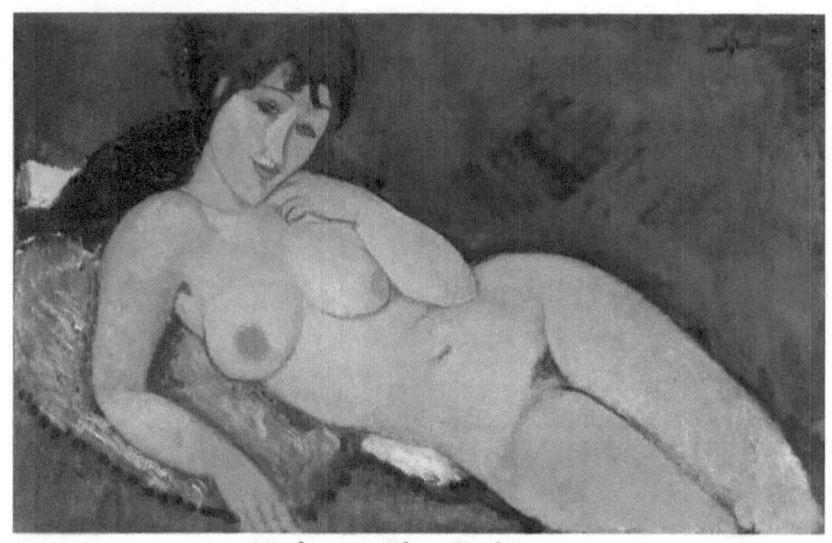

Nude on a Blue Cushion
1917, Oil on Canvas

MODIGLIANI

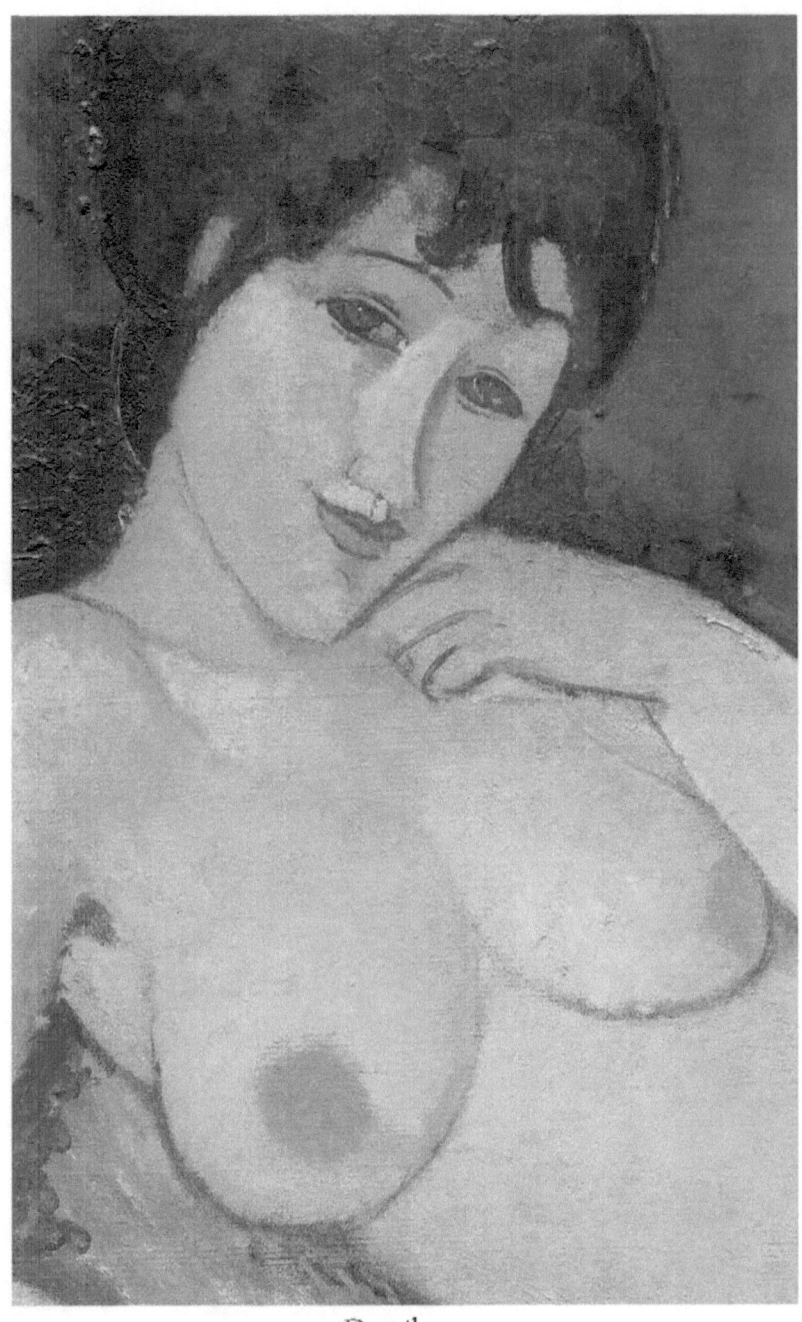

Detail

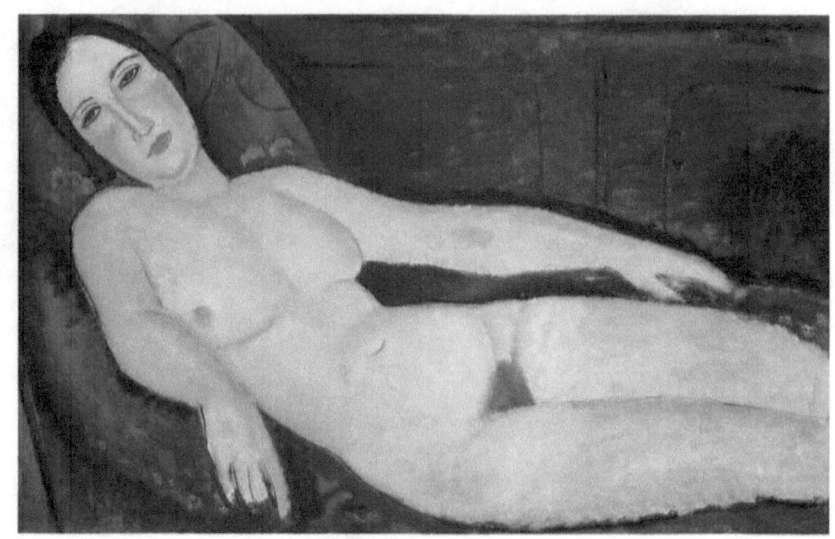

Nude on a Divan
1918, Oil on Canvas

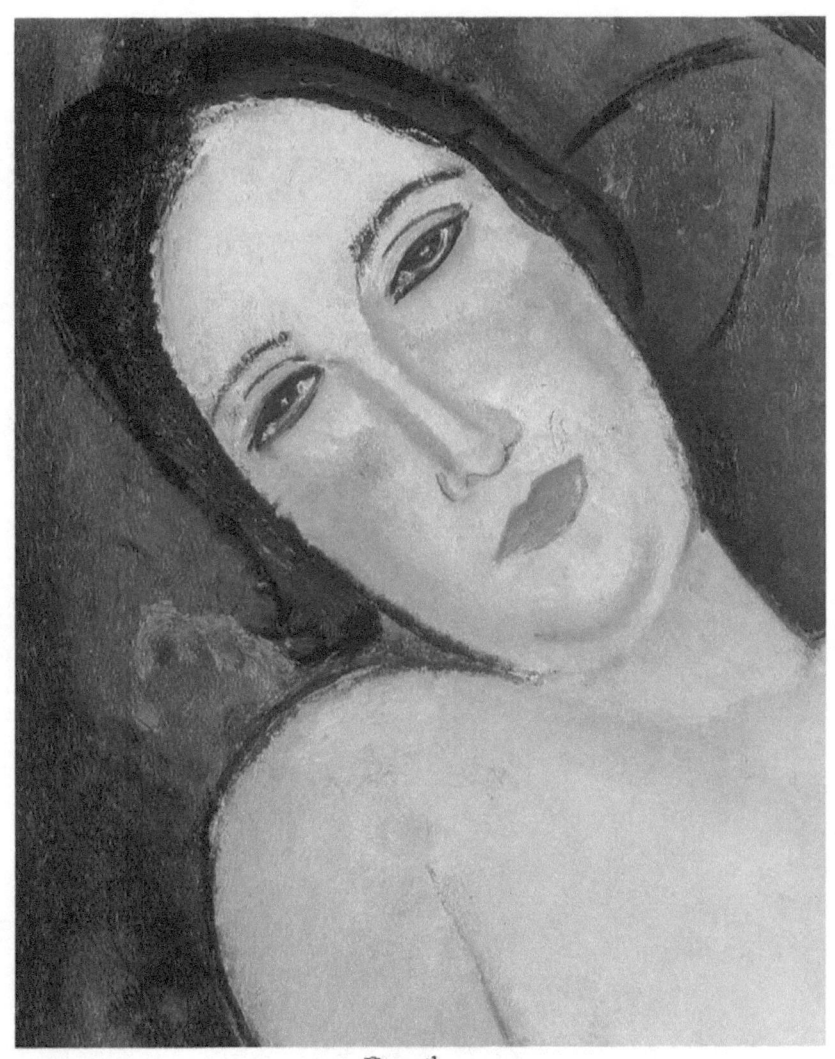

Detail

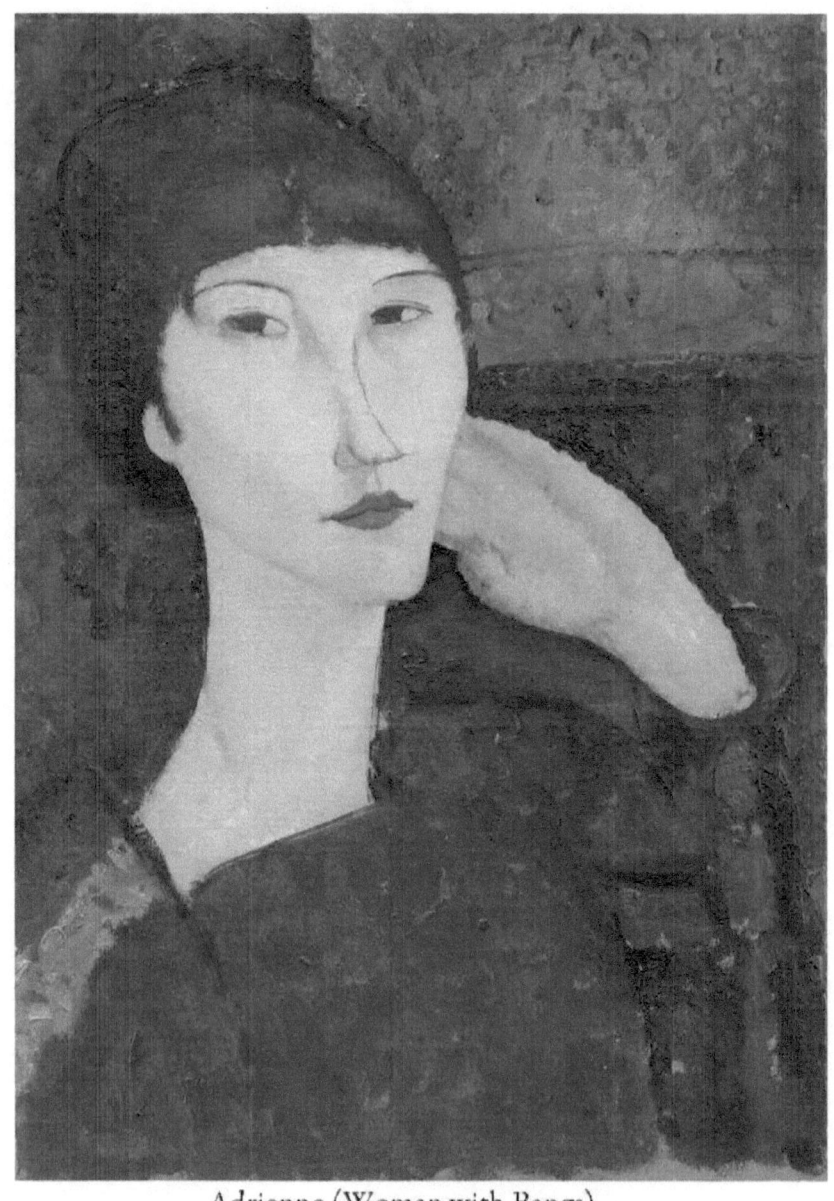

Adrienne (Woman with Bangs)
1917, Oil on Canvas

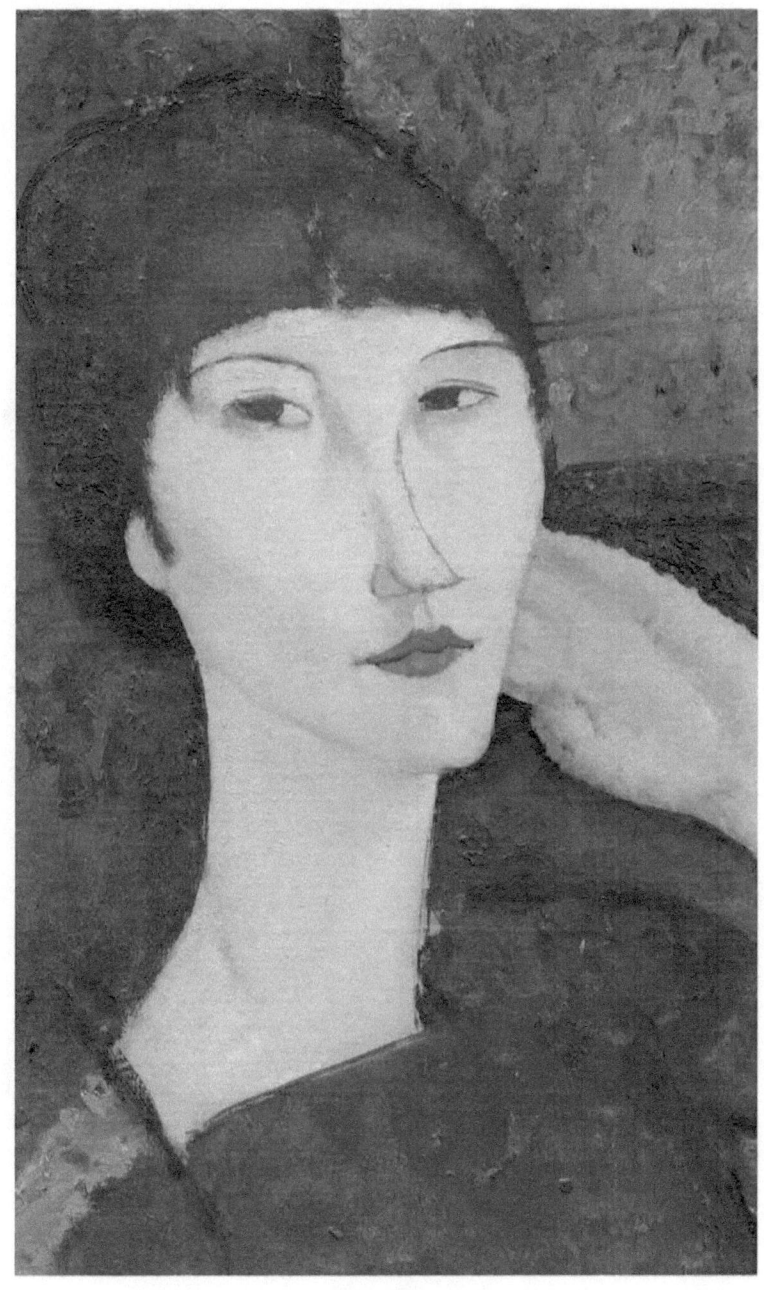

Detail

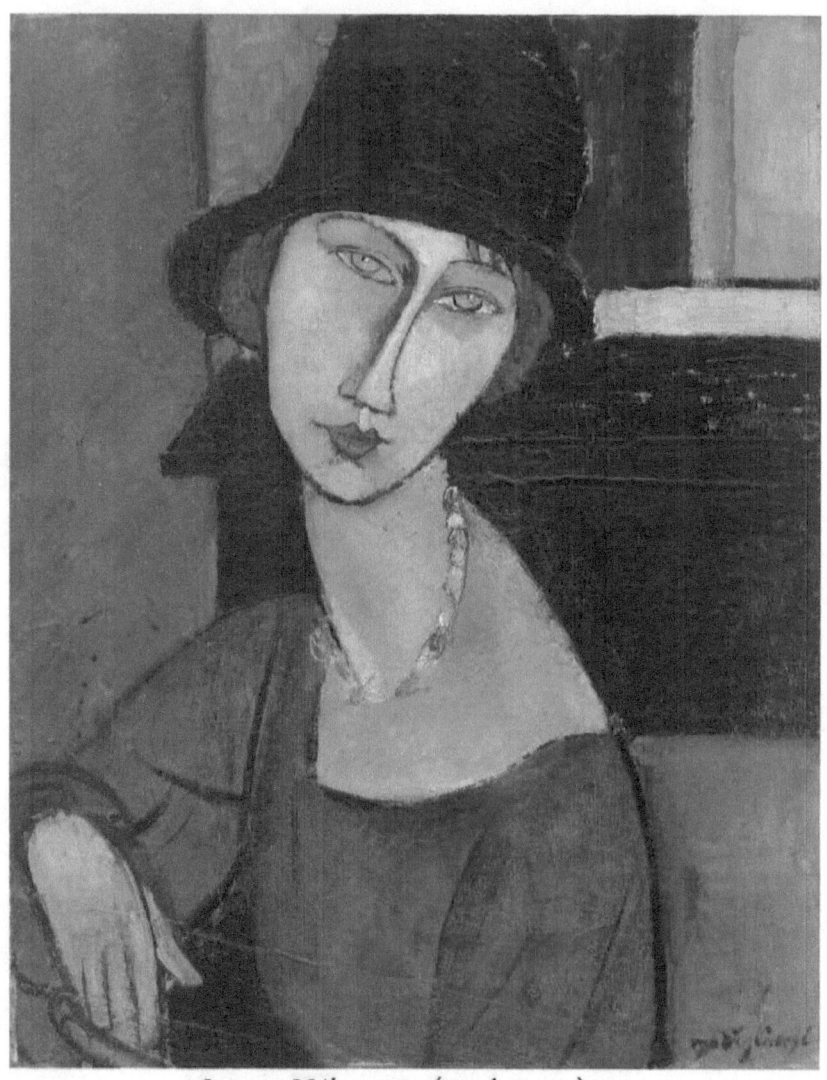

Jeanne Hébuterne (au chapeau)
1917, Oil on Canvas

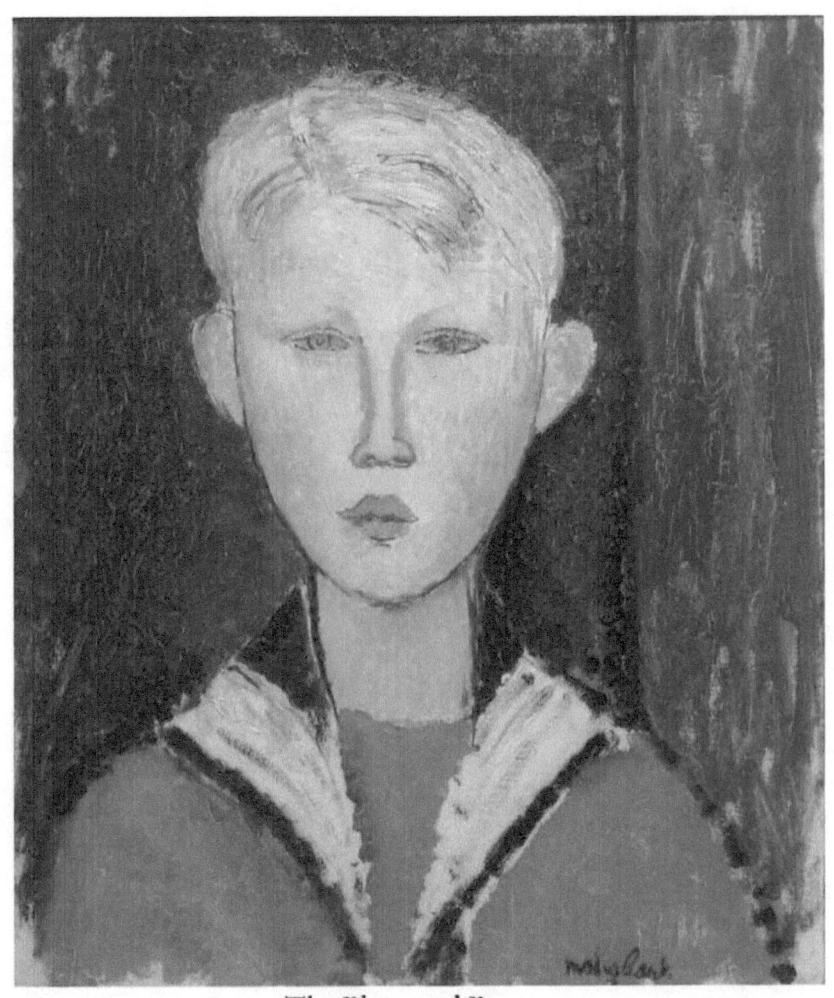

The Blue-eyed Boy
1917, Oil on Canvas

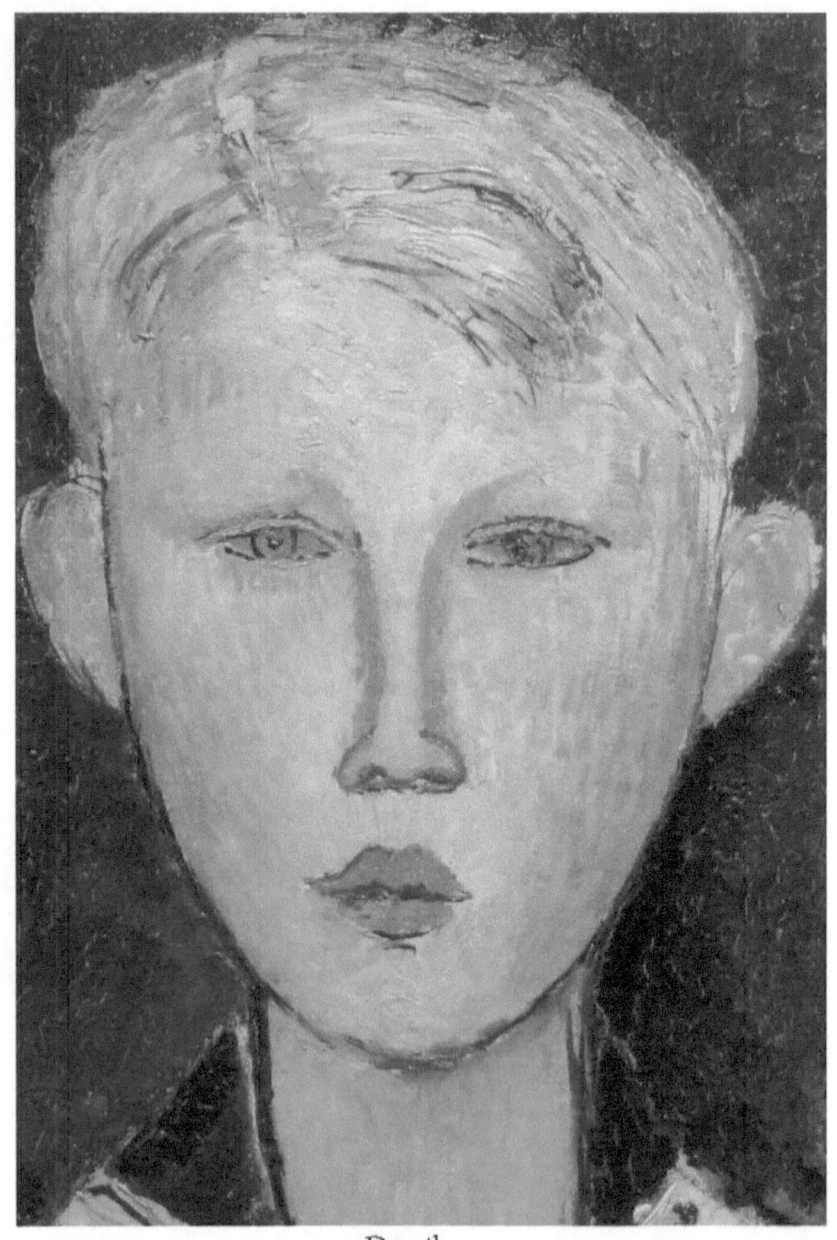

Detail

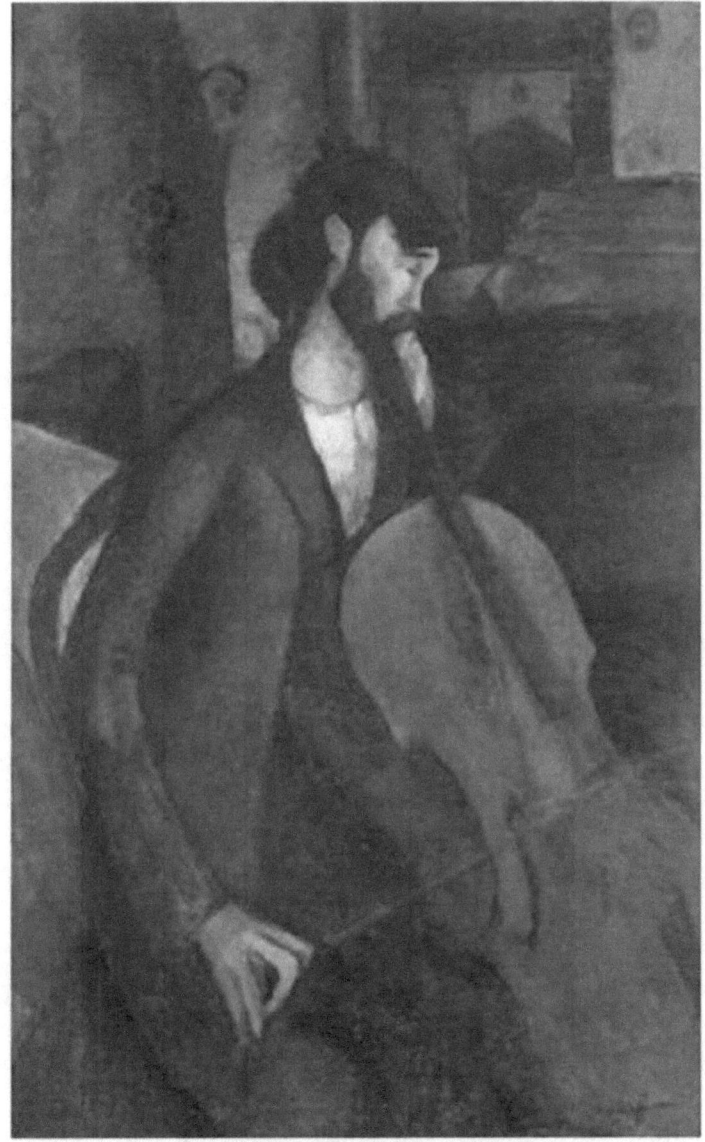

Le violoncelliste (The cellist)
1909, oil on canvas, 131 x 81 cm, Private Collection
Executed in 1909, Le violoncelliste is the finest achievement of
Modigliani's early career. Exquisitely composed, it represents the

culmination of a period in Modigliani's art that was characterized by the influence of Cezanne.

In the present work, Modigliani incorporates the lessons that he has learned from Cezanne and ultimately transcends them by resolving Cezanne's tonal harmonies and formal relationships into a more fluid and deliberately sculptural composition. When exhibited at the Salon des Indpendants in 1910, Le violoncelliste was famously acclaimed by Modigliani's friend and patron Dr. Paul Alexandre as being "better than Cezanne."

In addition to being Modigliani's ultimate statement on Cezanne, Le violoncelliste also marks the dawning in Modigliani's art of the artist's lifelong fascination with sculpture and in particular the influence of Brancusi. On his arrival in Paris in 1906, Modigliani had introduced himself around town as primarily a sculptor and shortly before he began work on Le violoncelliste in 1909, he had asked Dr. Paul Alexandre to introduce him to the famous Romanian sculptor. A long-time admirer of Brancusi's work, over the ensuing months the Romanian became both a significant influence on Modigliani's work and a close friend and substitute father-figure for the young Italian artist.

Brancusi was a shy man who seldom agreed to be photographed or painted, yet on the reverse of the oil study for Le violoncelliste there appears a rare portrait of Brancusi by Modigliani that remained unfinished. Many of the features of this portrait resemble those of Le violoncelliste and indeed it has been suggested that it is also a portrait of Brancusi, who though not known to have played the cello was a keen violinist and played regularly with the celebrated naive painter, Henri Rousseau. Despite the facial resemblance, the slender body and elongated forms of the figure in the painting are inconsistent with Brancusi's more robust figure.

The influence of Brancusi's elegant sculptural simplification of form on Modigliani during this period is nevertheless undeniable and can be most clearly witnessed in the smooth rounded and somewhat exaggerated forms of the cellist's features and in the carefully orchestrated spatial depth of the composition. Le violoncelliste was painted concurrently with a number of very sculptural paintings and drawings which, taking their inspiration from Brancusi and Cubism, attempt to convey three-dimensional form in two dimensions by means of highly stylized distortion.

Although Le violoncelliste is executed very much in the Cezanne-influenced style of his early work, it is not only Modigliani's earliest masterpiece but also the first of his paintings to clearly display the direction and character of the artist's later work.

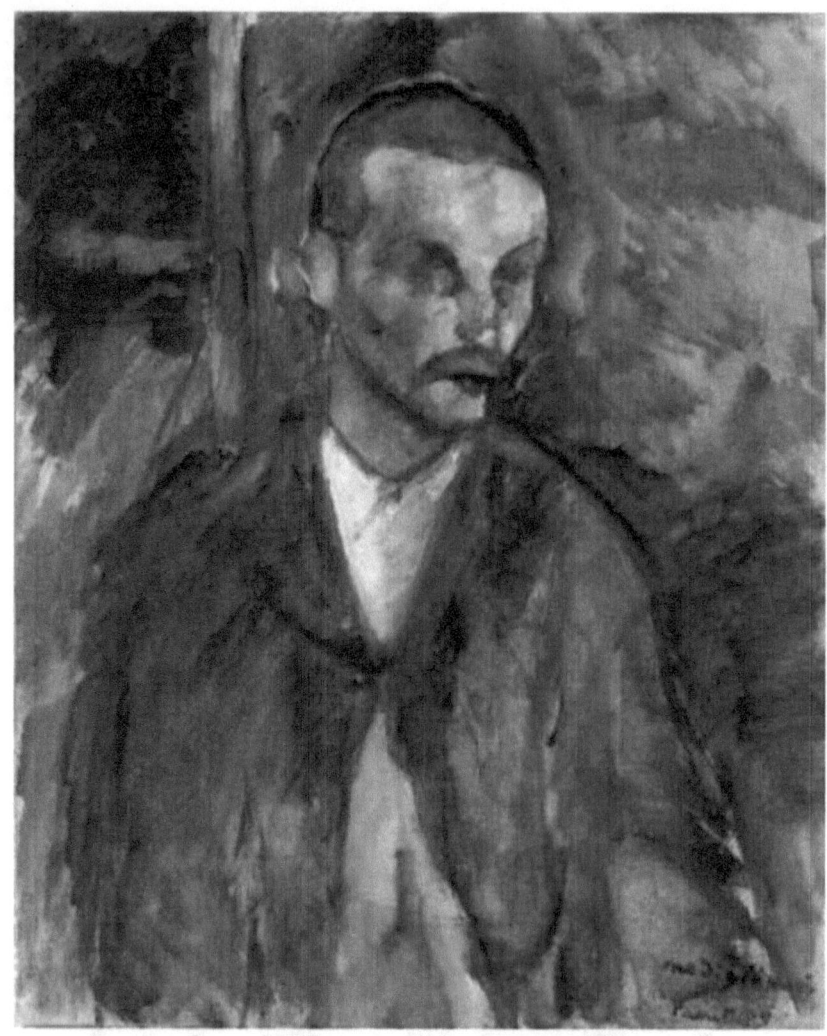

Le mendiant de Livourne (The Beggar of Livorno)
1909, oil on canvas, 65.8 x 52.4 cm, Private Collection

This was the only work painted during Modigliani's stay in Leghorn (July-September) that he was anxious to bring back to Paris. He is said to have kept it for several months on the wall of his Rue Falguière studio, before exhibiting it with several drawings and five other paintings at the Salon des Indépendants of 1910.

Cézanne had been the figurehead for an entire generation of painters, the last exhibition of his lifetime was at the 1906 Salon d'Automne, shortly after Modigliani's arrival in Paris and this picture, though painted at Leghorn, clearly shows his influence: the structure of the face and the strokes of intense color that punctuate its composition, the blue and green in particular, are particularly reminiscent of his style. Modigliani, apparently even made a small watercolor of Cézanne's Garçon au gilet rouge, 1888-90.

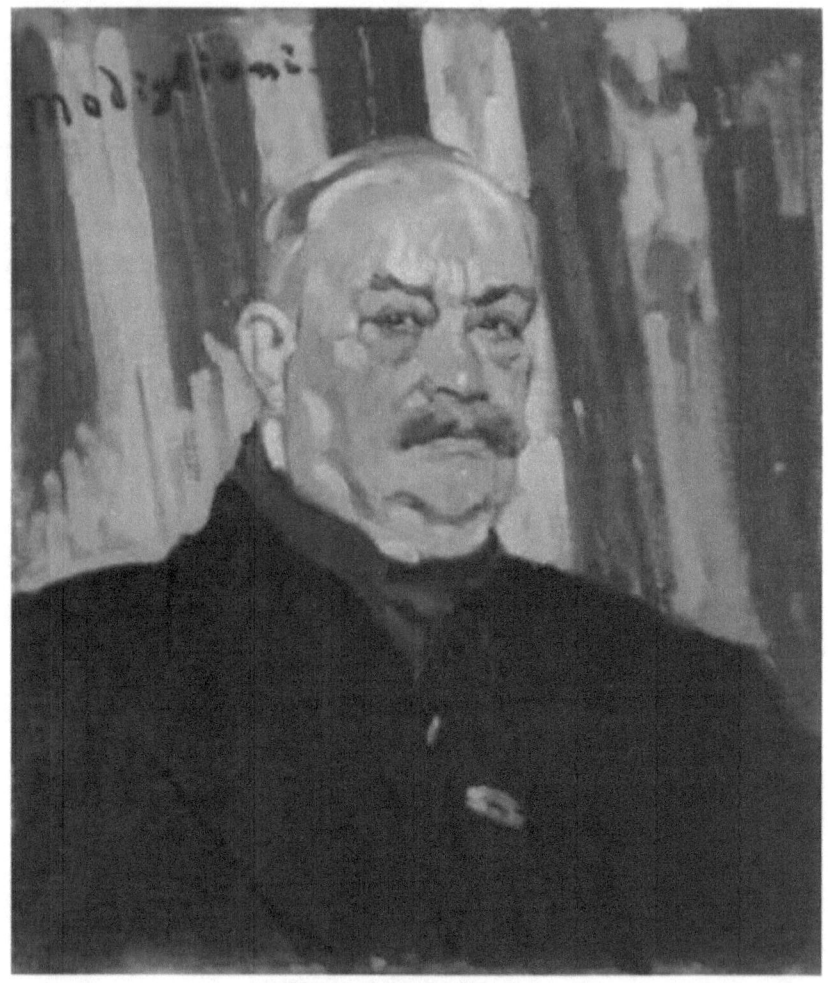

Portrait de Joseph Lévi

c. 1909, oil on canvas,. 55 x 46 cm, Private Collection

Painted circa 1909, Portrait de Joseph Lévi is an important early picture by Amedeo Modigliani, as is reflected by its extensive exhibition and publication history. The picture shows a fellow artist who also worked as a restorer, Joseph Lévi, and has remained in his family's collection since it was given to the sitter by the artist almost a century ago. Notwithstanding the forceful presence with which Modigliani invests the sitter, Lévi was a kindly man who often lent Modigliani money, a service that he would sometimes repay by giving him pictures; it appears that this may well have been one of the causes for the Bohemian artist to have painted this portrait of his older benefactor. It is telling of the importance of Lévi's friendship to Modigliani that he would come to execute a portrait of his son, Gaston, three years later, a picture which is now in the Denver Museum of Art.

The thick brushstrokes and bold color in the portrait of Lévi reveal the continued influence of the Fauve artists on Modigliani during this period. At the same time, there is a sculptural feel to the intense modeling of the facial features, perhaps hinting at Modigliani's acquaintance with the Romanian sculptor Constantin Brancusi, which began around the time that Portrait de Joseph Lévi was painted. This was the period when Modigliani forsook Montmartre for Montparnasse, the North for the South, and came into contact with a new circle of artists as well as keen collectors, patrons and enthusiasts such as Paul Alexandre. This encouraged Modigliani both in his revels and in his artistic experimentation, as he began to seek a new means of modeling form both in his pictures and in sculpture. Modigliani's search for a reduced and harmonious manner of rendering the world can already be discerned in the bold brushstrokes, the striped background and the simplification of form in Portrait de Joseph Lévi.

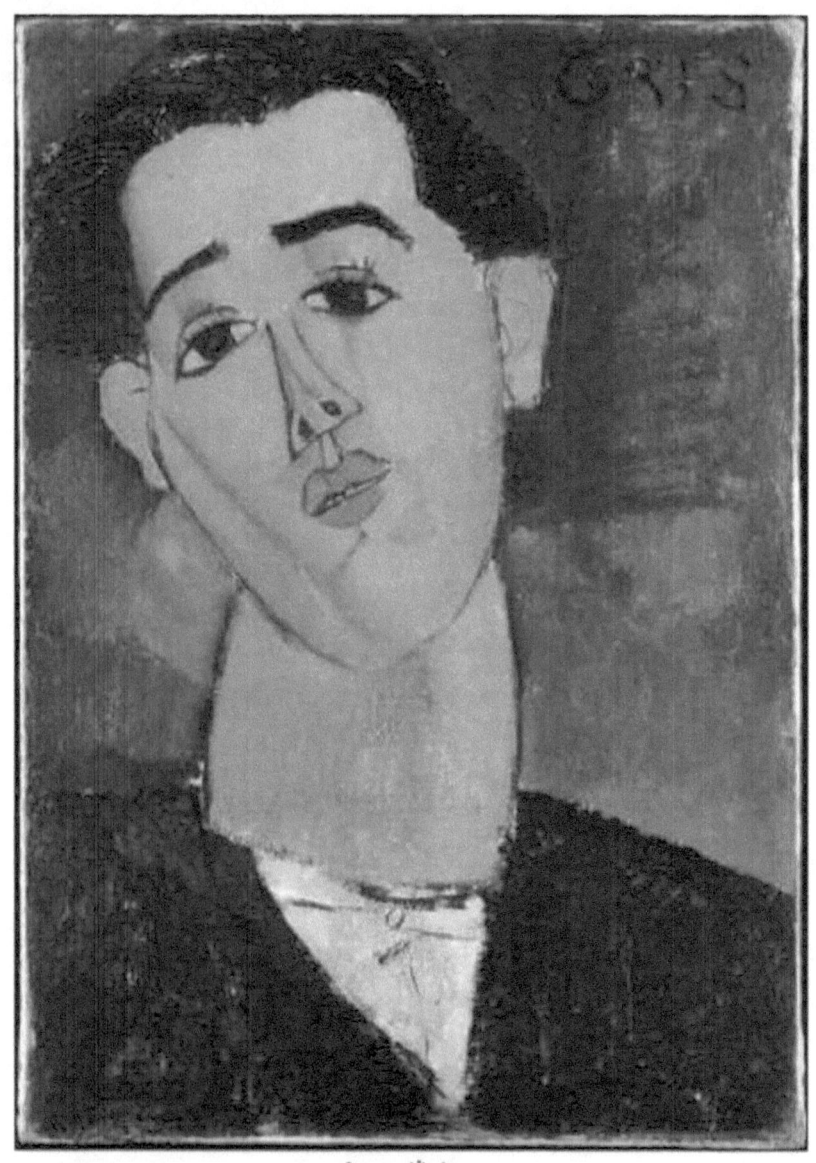

Juan Gris
1915. Oil on canvas. (54.9 x 38.1 cm. The Metropolitan
Museum of Art

MODIGLIANI

José Victoriano González-Pérez, better known as Juan Gris, was a Spanish painter and sculptor who lived and worked in France most of his life. His works, which are closely connected to the emergence of an innovative artistic genre — Cubism — are among the movement's most distinctive. In 1906 he moved to Paris and became friends with Henri Matisse, Georges Braque, Fernand Léger, then in 1915 he was painted by his friend, Amedeo Modigliani.

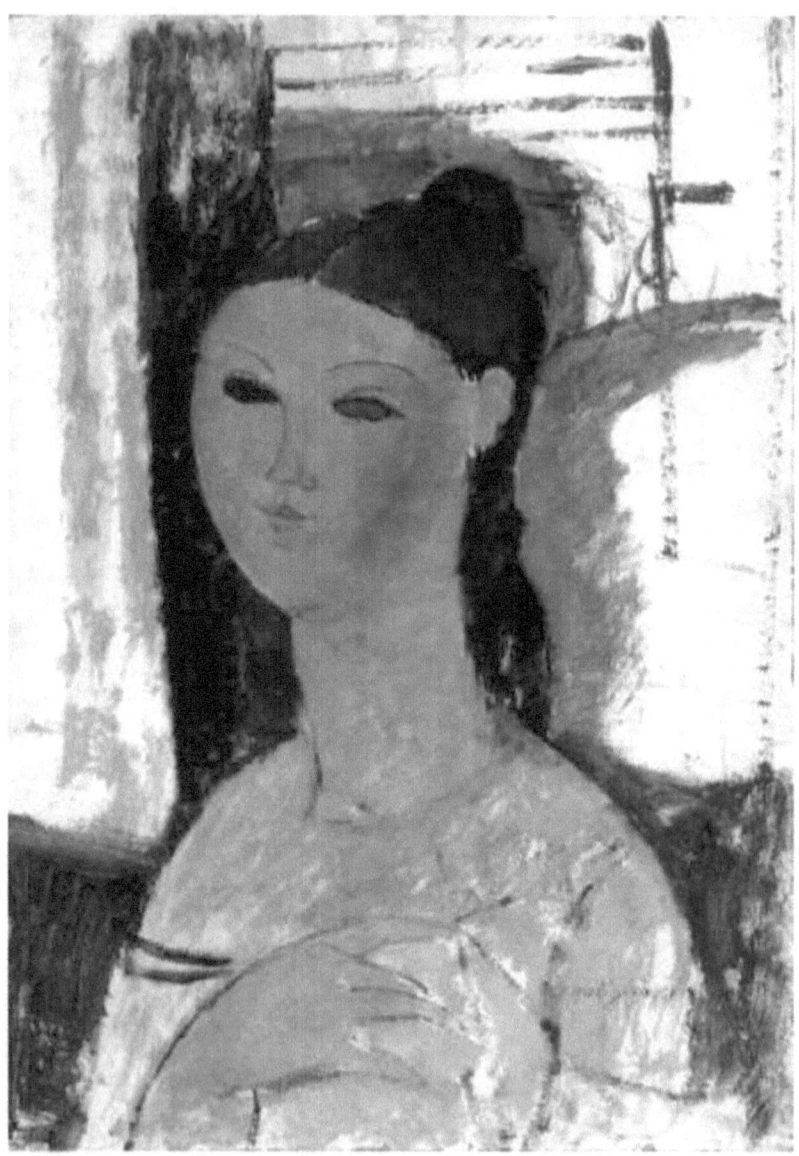

Portrait of a young woman, seated
c. 1915, oil on card. 75.0 x 52.4. cm. Tate Gallery, London
Subject formerly identified as Beatrice Hasting, although the
features bear little resemblance with other portraits of her by

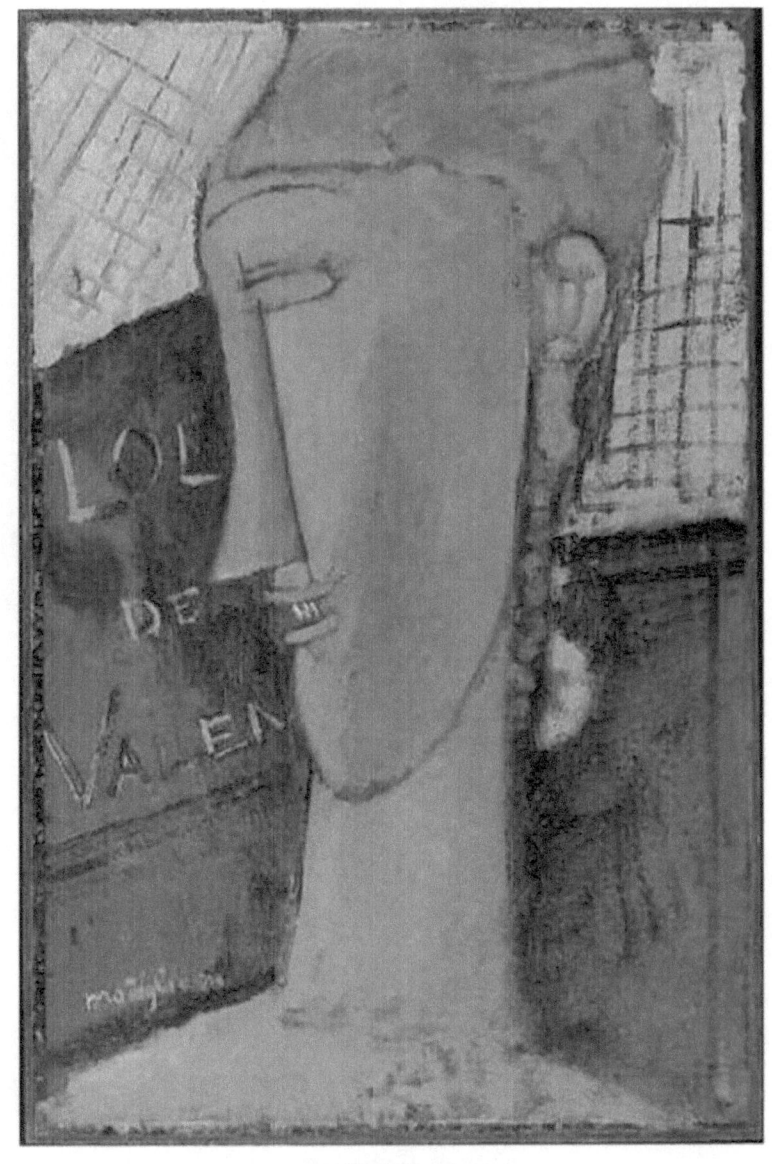

Lola de Valence
1915, Oil on paper, mounted on wood, 50.8 x 33.7 cm, The
Metropolitan Museum of Art

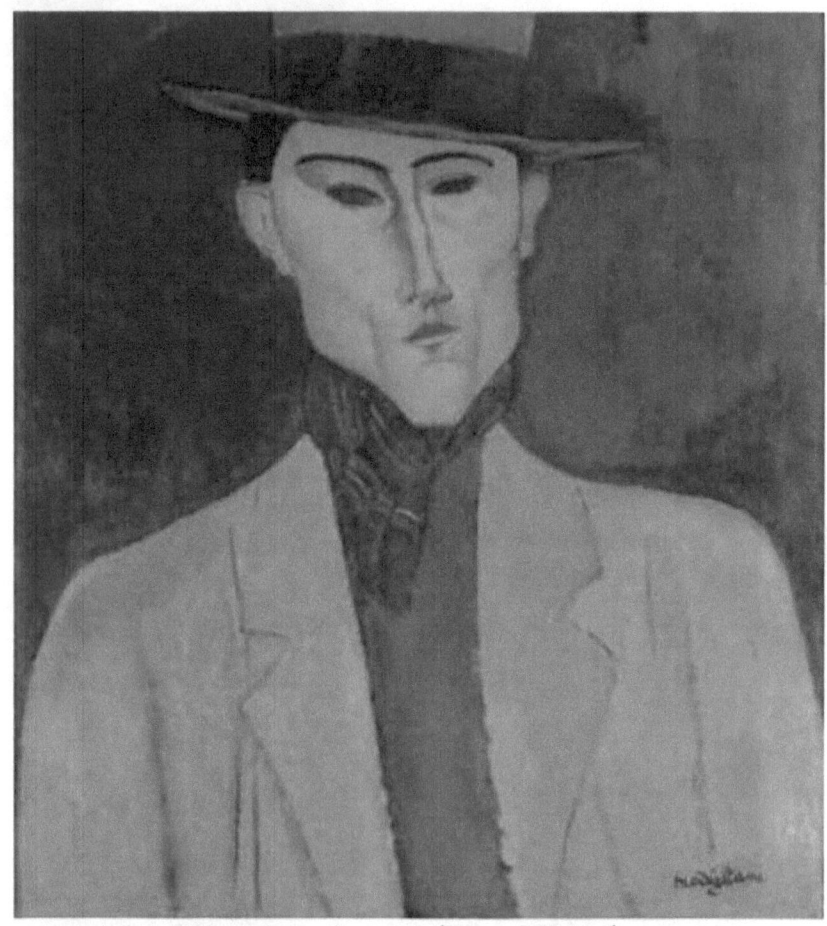

Homme au chapeau (Man with hat)
1915, oil on canvas, 65 x 54 cm, Private Collection

For Modigliani, sculpture had been a vocation, and yet his health meant that he was physically unable to withstand the level of exertion that work in stone - the only sculptural medium that he truly believed in - demanded from him. He returned, then, to painting, but his experiences as a sculptor came to flavor his work, giving them their unique sense of modeling - a factor that is so vividly evident in the face of the Homme au chapeau. These characteristics would come to result in the increasing sense of accomplishment and therefore the consequent popularity of his pictures from the period.

Modigliani's portraits often introduce this sculptural sense of the three-dimensional to the face, but deliberately suppress it in the rest of the painting. In Homme au chapeau, this is clear both in the dark background and also in the clothes that he is wearing. This flatness contrasts heavily with the finely modeled face, an effect that is heightened by the difference that exists even in terms of the textures of the paint in the various areas. Where the lines of the jacket are marked with simplicity, those of the face have been carefully applied with an acute appreciation of the modulation of tone. This is especially evident in the depiction of the subject's nose, where thin, sharp lines have been used to evoke perfectly the shape and form. In addition, the deft manipulation of shade, in the lower half of the face, shows us that the sitter's face is inclined and somewhat unshaven.

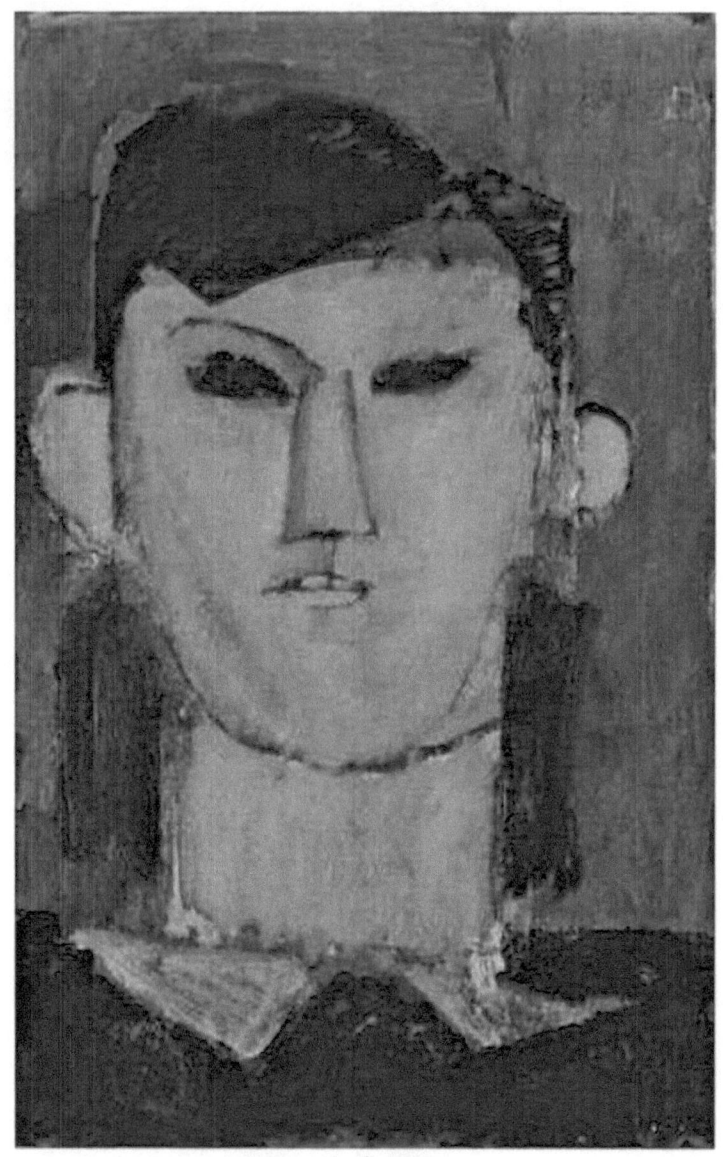

Portrait de Picasso
1915, oil on paper laid down on card, canvas backed, 34.2 x
26.3cm, Private Collection

Picasso and Modigliani both had a great respect for each other's artistic abilities, Modigliani referred to Picasso as "always being ten years ahead of the rest of us". This portrait of Picasso is one of a series of portraits of his fellow artists Modigliani painted in 1915. Following the 1914 portraits of F. B. Haviland and Diego Rivera in 1915.

By this time Montparnasse had been discovered by artists from all parts of the world. It had superseded Montmartre as the centre for intellectual life. The Closerie des Lilas, as well as the two famous cafés, La Rotonde and Le Dôme, were the meeting places for painters and poets who often engaged in heated discussion with political exiles such as Trotsky. Artists returning from the front could find their friends in those café terraces. Writing about the atmosphere, Roland Penrose recalled, "The company was widely international, those in uniform such as Léger, Raynal, Braque, Derain, Apollinaire and many others mixed again with painters, sculptors and writers such as Modigliani, Kisling, Severini, Soffici, Chirico, Lipchitz, Archipenko, Brancusi, Cendrars, Reverdy, Salmon, Dalize. There was no lack of talent among them..." (Picasso: His Life and Work, London, 1958, p. 193).

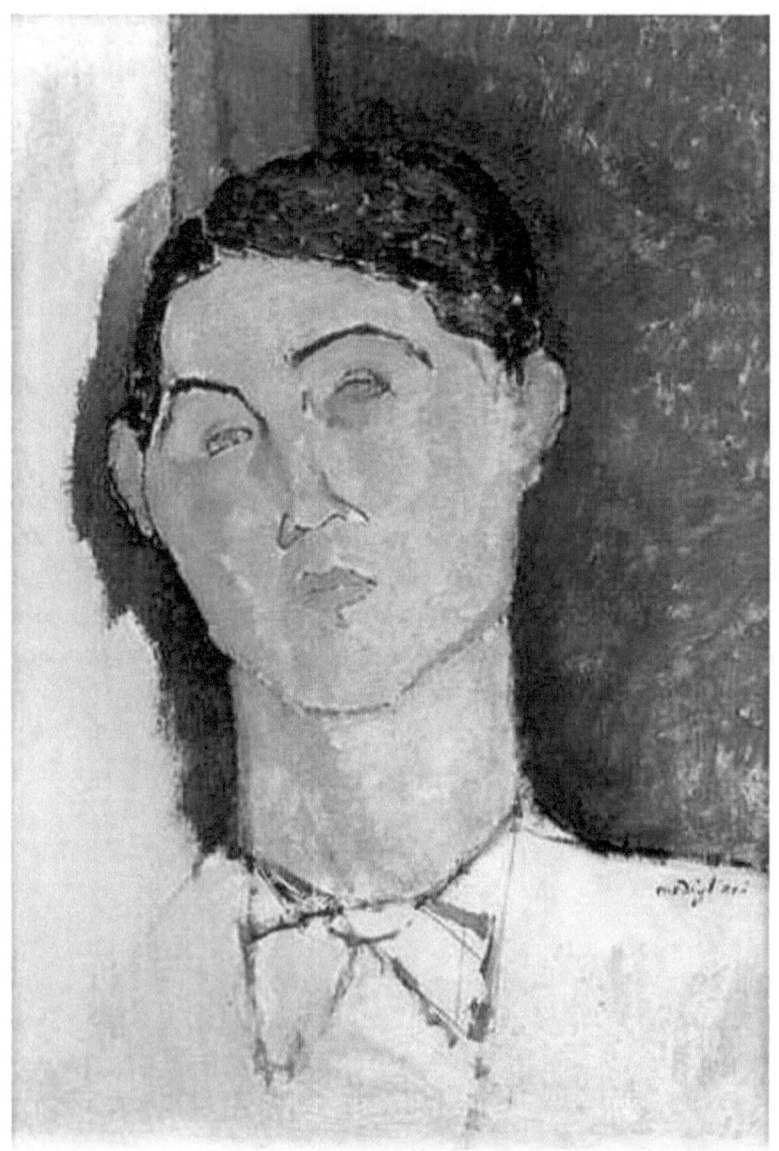

Head of young man
1916. oil and pencil on board. 55.9 x 39.3cm. Private
Collection

Painted circa 1916, the present picture has been identified as a portrait of Conrad Moricand. Conrad Moricand was a writer and artist, and a close friend of Modigliani. It was Moricand, who along with Kisling, had made a clumsy attempt to take the death-mask of Modigliani after the latter's untimely death in 1920; his efforts had to be rescued from disaster by the sculptor Lipchitz.

Henry Miller gives an interesting account of Moricand in his book A Devil in Paradise: "Moricand was not only an astrologer and a scholar steeped in the hermetic philosophies, but an occultist. In appearance there was something of the mage (sic) about him. Rather tall, well built, broad shouldered, heavy and slow in his movements he might have been taken for the descendant of an American Indian family. He liked to think, he later confided, that there was a connection between the name Moricand and Mohican. ... He was an incurable dandy living the life of a beggar." (H. Miller, A Devil in Paradise, 1956, p. 6).

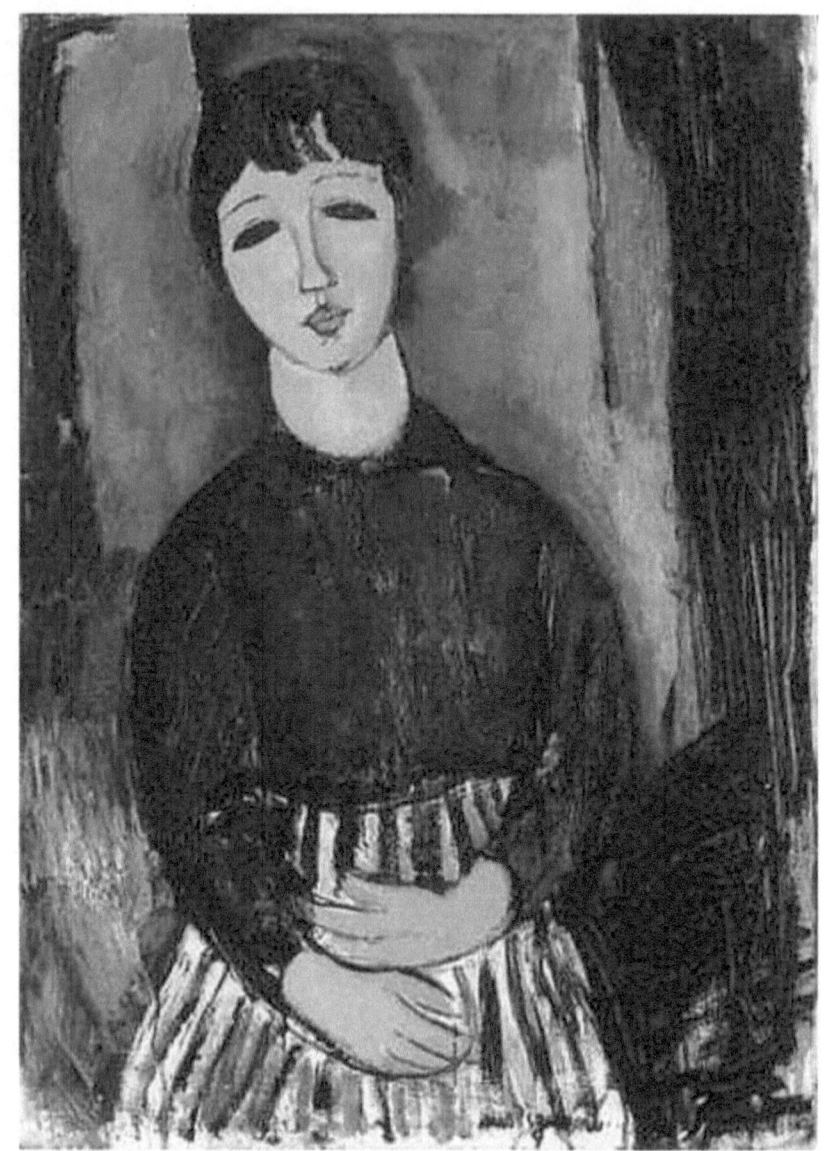

La servante au tablier ray (The servant in apron ray)
1916, oil on canvas, 92 x 64.8 cm. Private Collection

More than any other artist of the early twentieth century, Modigliani concentrated on portraiture as his principal medium of creativity. The present work, painted in 1916, is a masterpiece from Modigliani's first period of full artistic maturity.

Jacques Lipchitz, the sculptor, wrote a short book on Modigliani. An intimate friend of the painter, he commissioned Modigliani to do a wedding portrait of Lipchitz and his wife. He has left a fascinating account of Modigliani's working procedure: He preferred painting on a closely woven canvas, and sometimes when he had finished the work he placed a sheet of paper carefully over the fresh paint to merge the colors. He worked without an easel and with the minimum fuss, placing his canvas on a chair and painting quietly. From time to time he would get up and glance critically over his work and look at his models. According to Lipchitz, Modigliani charged 10 francs and a bottle of wine per sitting. Other artists and clients testify that Modigliani always drank as he worked. Lipchitz has written the best analysis of Modigliani's methods and style:

"His own art was an art of personal feeling. He worked furiously, dashing off drawing after drawing without stopping to correct and ponder. He worked, it seemed, entirely by instinct - which, however, was extremely fine and sensitive, perhaps owing much to his Italian inheritance and his love of the early Renaissance masters. He could not forget his interest in people, and he painted them, so to say, with abandon."

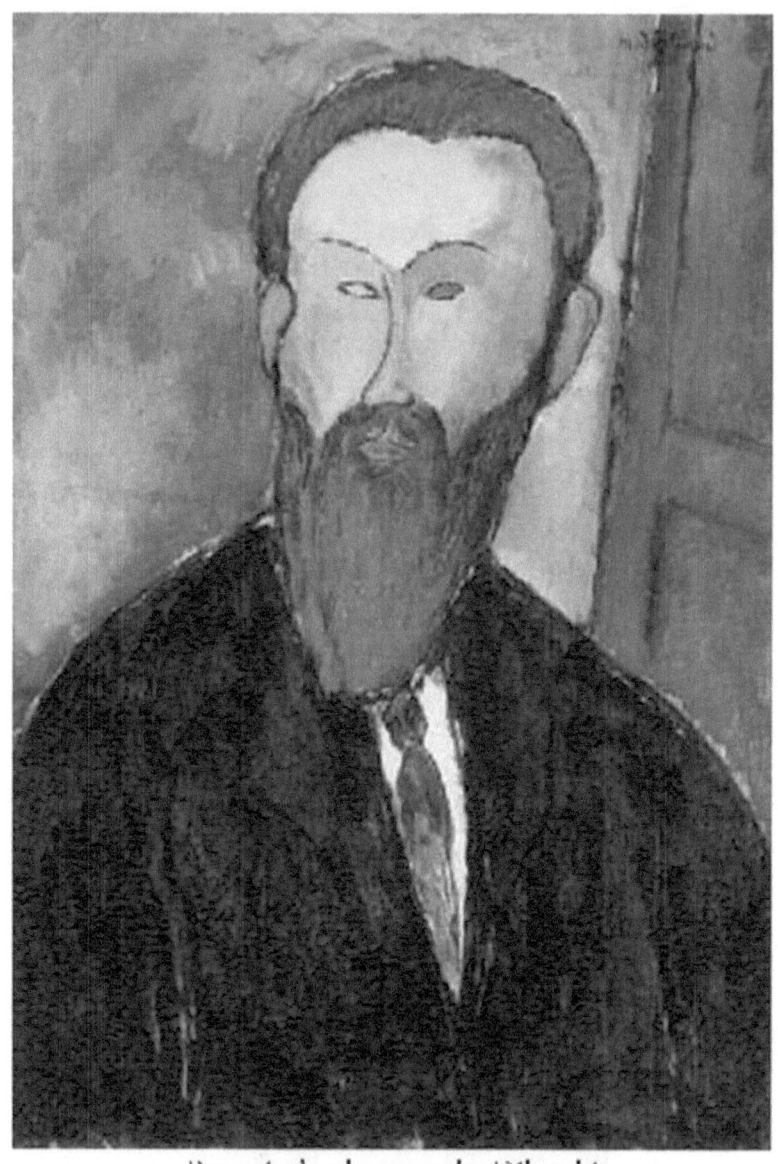

Portrait du photographe Dilewski
1916, oil on canvas, 73 x 50.2 cm, Private Collection

Around 1916, Modigliani made the acquaintance of the art dealer Paul Guillaume and celebrated his first one-man exhibition at the Berthe Weill Gallery the following year.

The Jewish artists of Montparnasse often gathered at the Café de la Rotonde, on the corner of the newly opened boulevard Raspail and the boulevard du Montparnasse. In addition to Chaim Soutine, Marc Chagall, Chana Orloff, Ossip Zadkine, Moïse Kisling, Jules Pascin and Jacques Lipchitz, the café was also frequented by non-Jewish artists, such as Pablo Picasso, André Salmon, Diego Rivera, Max Jacob, Maurice de Vlaminck and Fernand Léger. These luminaries of the circle of Montparnasse comprised Modigliani's intimate circle of friends.

Modigliani's portraits form a kind of visual history of Left Bank culture dating back to the war years. His sitters included: Max Jacob; the critic and art dealer Adolphe Basler; Paul Guillaume; Léon Indenbaum; the sculptor Chana Orloff; the painter Pincus Krémègne; Henri Laurens; Constantin Brancusi, with whom he worked in 1911-1912; Diego Rivera; Frank Haviland Burty; Pablo Picasso; Jacques Lipchitz, Moïse Kisling; and the photographer Dilewski.

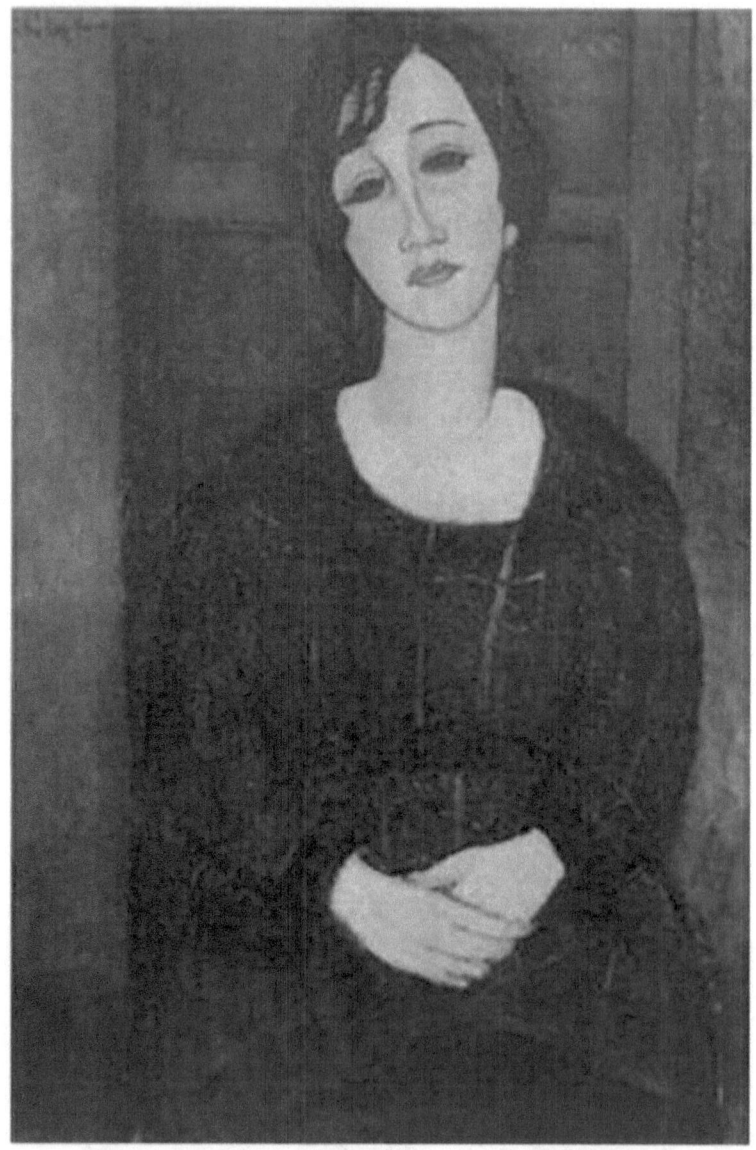

Femme en robe cossaise (Woman in Plaid Dress)
1916, oil on canvas. 92 x 60 cm. Private Collection

More than any other artist of the early twentieth century,
Modigliani concentrated on portraiture as his principal vehicle of

creativity. The present work, painted in 1916, is a masterpiece from Modigliani's first period of full artistic maturity. The picture reveals both the key sources of the artist's style, and the unique and original synthesis he made of them.

The first influence manifest in the present work is Cezanne. Modigliani adored the pictures of the French painter, and talked passionately of his admiration for them. It is perhaps not an accident that so many of Modigliani's sitters are posed in an armchair with their hands clasped in their laps in the manner of Cezanne's portraits of his wife.

The second major influence on Modigliani was the sculptor Brancusi, whom Modigliani met through Dr. Paul Alexandre. In response to the impact of Brancusi's art, between 1909 and 1912 Modigliani concentrated on sculpture; the older artist's emphasis on geometric form became a permanent part of Modigliani's aesthetic.

The third influence evident in the present work is African sculpture. The stylized head of the woman, with the almond shaped eyes and the impassive and yet moving expression, was clearly based in part on masks from the Dan tribe. It is striking that Paul Guillaume, Modigliani's principal dealer before June 1916, was also the most important dealer of African sculpture in Paris, who organized a contemporaneous exhibition that paired Modigliani's paintings paired with African masks.

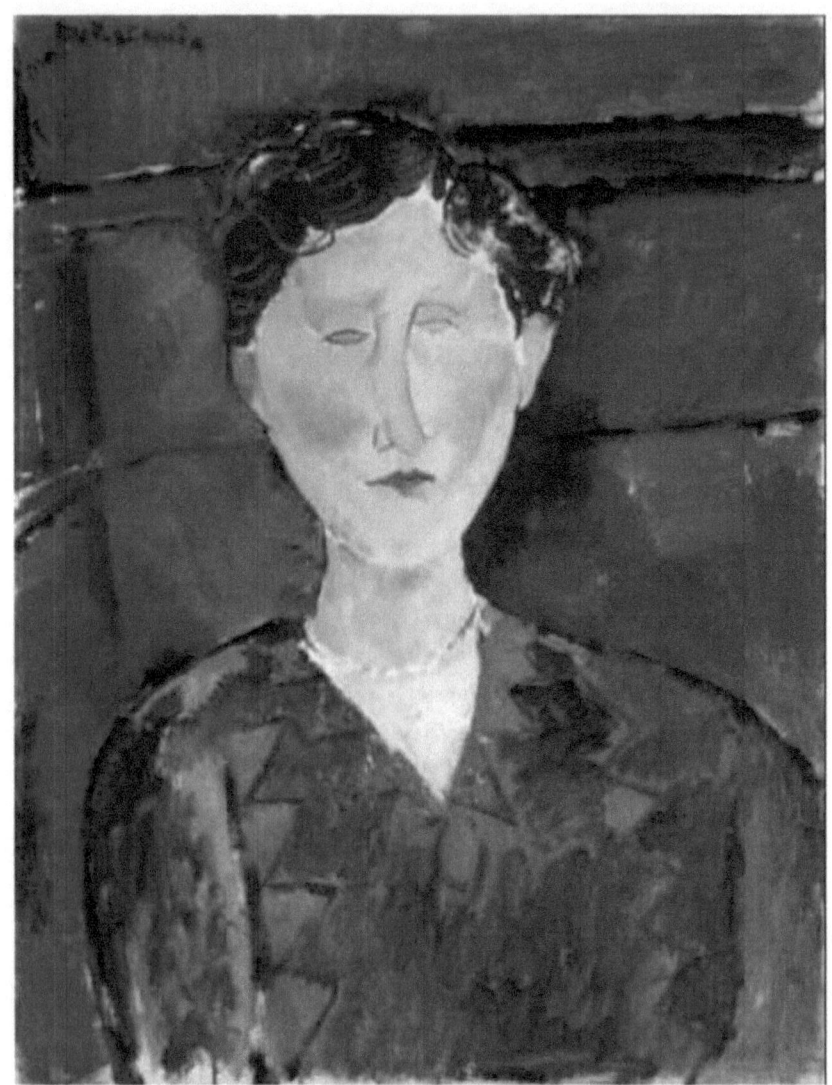

Portrait de femme au corsage bleu (Portrait of woman in blue blouse)
c. 1916, Oil on canvas, 61 x 45 cm, Private Collection
The strong sculptural elements seen in the rendering of this portrait are reminiscent of the artist's stone heads of 1911-1912 and more importantly, reflect his exploration of Cubism from the

study of Picasso's early Cubist paintings. Picasso and Modigliani became friends soon after Modigliani's 1906 arrival in Paris. Picasso's portraits of his mistress Fernande Olivier executed during 1908-1909 depict her face as a series of fractured planes, and works such as these were influential in the development of Modigliani's own work. While Portrait de femme au corsage bleu exhibits a more naturalistic rendering of the face, Modigliani emphasized the temples and cheeks of the face to create a highly modulated surface.

The works of Paul Cézanne were another seminal influence in the artist's development. The present picture is strongly reminiscent of Cézanne's portraits of Madame Cézanne seated in front of a interior wall, such as Madame Cézanne au fauteuil jaune, 1888-1890. The composition of Portrait de femme au corsage bleu exhibits a similar treatment of the face, shown in asymmetrical features and brushstrokes of color defining the planes of the face.

Building on the influences of Picasso and Cézanne, Modigliani created a unique style of portraiture that utilizes a deeply hued palette, rich impasto, and linear drawing. While he incorporated external influences into his work, Modigliani based his portraits on keen observation of the sitter and their attributes. In the present work, the sitter's calm demeanor and tasteful wardrobe are clearly evident; however, the individualizing characteristics have been transformed and rendered immortal by the artist.

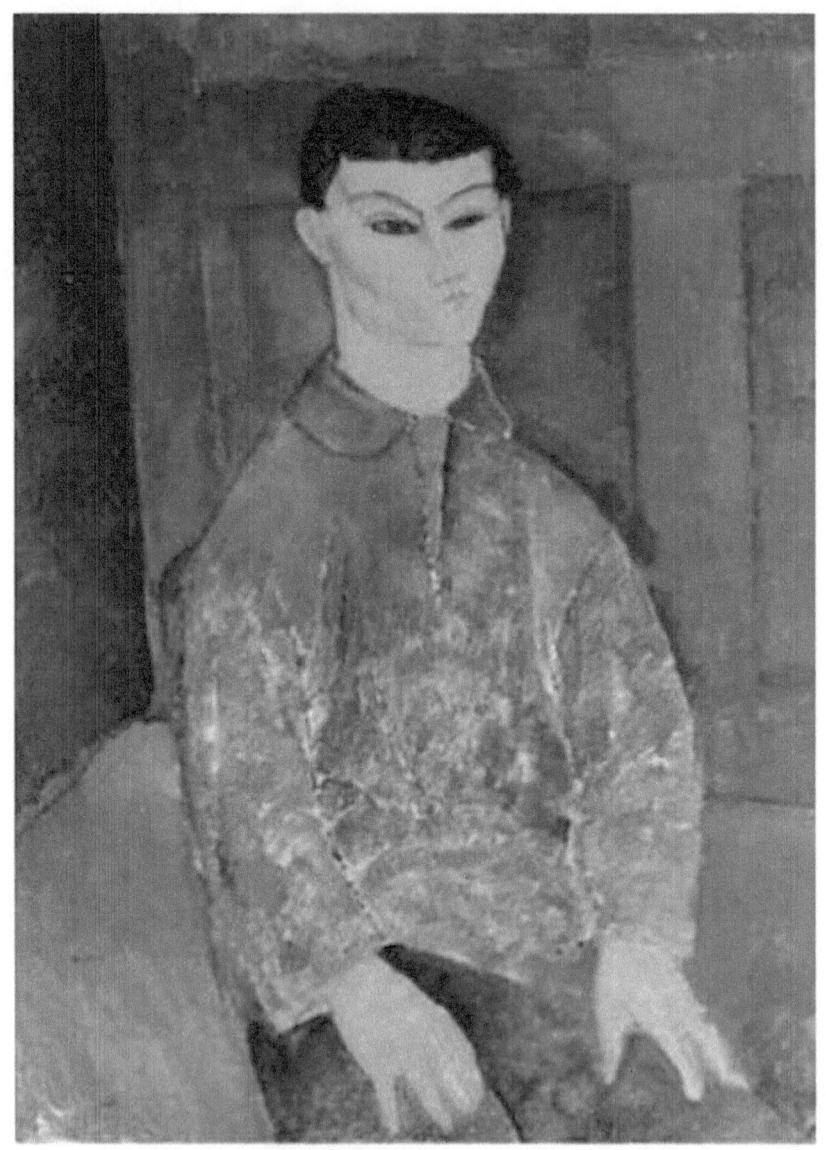

Moïse Kisling seduto (Moïse Kisling sitting)
1916, oil on board, 104.8 x 74.9 cm, Private Collection
The present painting is the largest of three portraits that
Modigliani made of one of his closest friends, the Polish artist

Moïse Kisling . Painted in 1915 and 1916, these images of Kisling are part of an important group of several dozen portraits by Modigliani that depict the artists, writers, dealers, and collectors who frequented bohemian Montparnasse during the war years. Taken together, these paintings constitute a veritable visual history of Left Bank culture in the second decade of the twentieth century.

When Modigliani moved to Montparnasse from neighboring Montmartre in late 1908 or early 1909, the neighborhood had already earned a reputation as the center of avant-garde artistic life in Paris. Lively, cosmopolitan, and sophisticated, Montparnasse was home to hundreds of artists and writers from dozens of different countries. The Café de la Rotonde, situated on the Boulevard du Montparnasse, functioned as the principal gathering place for this group, which included Picasso, Juan Gris, Diego Rivera, Chaïm Soutine, Jacques Lipchitz, and Max Jacob, among many others.

Moïse Kisling, the subject of the present portrait, was another of the most popular figures in Montparnasse during this period . Born in Poland in 1891, he studied at the Kraków School of Fine Arts until 1910, when he moved to Paris. He settled at 3, rue Joseph Bara, a building occupied almost entirely by painters and sculptors.

Extroverted and generous, Kisling loved to play host, and his studio soon emerged as a favorite haunt for avant-garde artists, much like Picasso's apartment at the Bateau-Lavoir had been during the previous decade. Kisling also became one of Modigliani's closest friends and staunchest supporters. Starting in 1916, he shared his studio with Modigliani, even supplying the perennially impoverished painter with canvas and pigment. The two artists were frequently spotted together in the cafés and watering holes of the Left Bank, and a drawing by the Russian artist Maria Marevna shows them reveling with Soutine in Diego Rivera's studio in Montparnasse . In his biography of Modigliani, Pierre Sichel writes, "Less volatile than Modi, Kisling played as hard as he worked, chased the girls, drank, enjoyed parties and good times, but never became unhinged in the process. His exuberance and his magnificent gestures endeared him to Modigliani. There was the time he sold a painting for a hundred francs. Then, walking along the street with Modi, he spent all hundred on flowers which he impulsively gave to the women passing by—not just to pretty women, but to the ordinary, the young, the old, the beautiful, the ugly"

The present portrait is a striking character study of the young Kisling, depicted at the age of twenty-five. It shows him seated on a chair or stool, his hands in his lap and his torso turned at a slight three-quarter angle. In the background is what appears to be either a paneled door or the stretcher for a large canvas, propped upright against the wall. Kisling is clad in a blue artist's smock and simple, dark trousers. His expression is reserved yet guileless, and his posture is slightly ungainly. The physiognomic details of the portrait are unmistakably Kisling's, especially the wide brow with its thick fringe of dark hair.

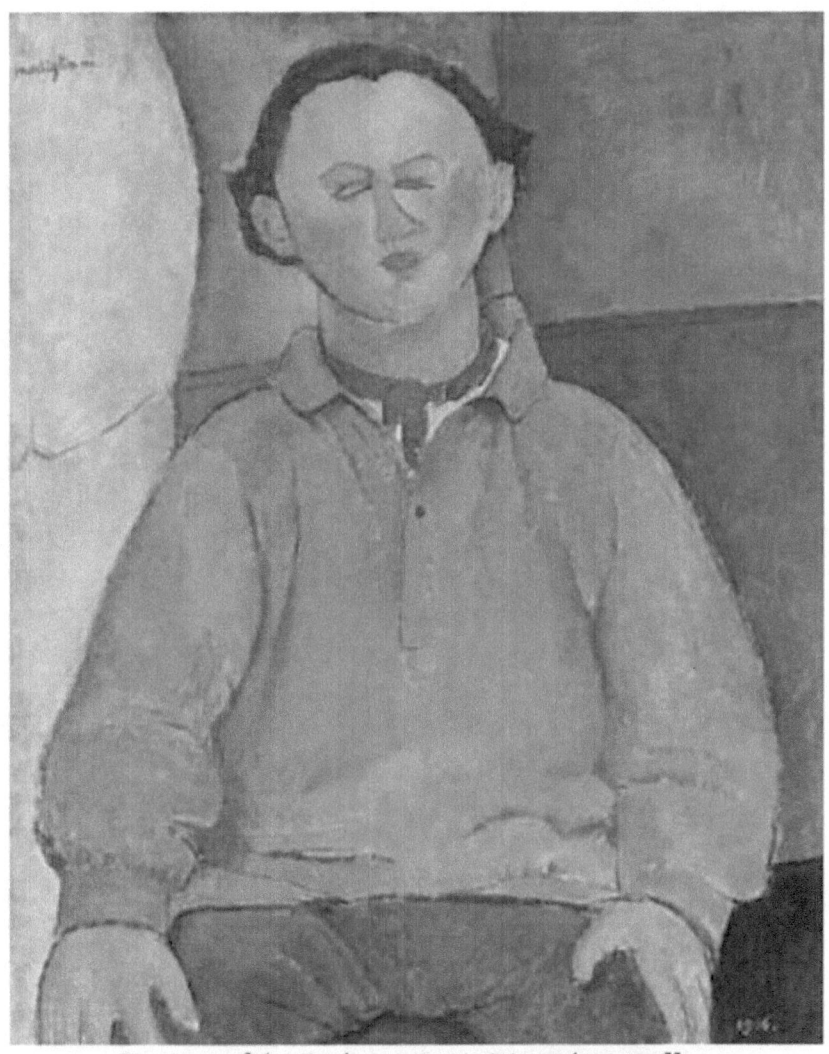

Portrait of the Sculptor Oscar Miestchaninoff
Painted in 1916, oil on canvas, 81.2 x 65 cm, private Collection
Depicting the sculptor Oscar Miestchaninoff, the present painting is one of an important group of several dozen portraits by Modigliani that record the artists, writers, dealers, and collectors who frequented bohemian Montparnasse during the war years.

Taken together, these works constitute a veritable visual history of Left Bank culture in the second decade of the twentieth century

Oscar Miestchaninoff, the subject of the present portrait, was the son of a Jewish shopkeeper from the Russian town of Vitebsk. Born in 1886, Miestchaninoff studied sculpture briefly at the Odessa School of Fine Arts before moving to Paris in 1909. He took an apartment in the Cité Falguière, an important artists' residence in Montparnasse, with numerous ground-floor studios that appealed especially to sculptors. Modigliani, who devoted himself almost exclusively to sculpture between 1909 and 1914, was already living at the Cité Falguière when Miestchaninoff arrived, and it is likely that the two artists met shortly thereafter. Miestchaninoff worked in a classicizing style and was one of the few non-Cubist artists whom Modigliani painted. He briefly attended classes at the École des Arts Décoratifs and the École des Beaux-Arts before enrolling in the Académie Russe, an independent artists' academy in Montparnasse that catered especially to Russian émigrés.

In the evenings, the Académie hosted open sketching sessions from a live model, which both Modigliani and Miestchaninoff's close friend Soutine are known to have frequented. Although his work is little known today, Miestchaninoff enjoyed a degree of professional and financial success during his lifetime, frequently exhibiting with other Jewish artists. He moved to the United States during World War II and remained there until his death in 1956.

The present painting is striking character study of the Russian sculptor, depicted at the age of thirty. It shows him seated with his hands firmly planted on his lap, a pose that recalls both Ingres's Monsieur Bertin and Picasso's famous 1906 portrait of Gertrude Stein (the latter painted while both Picasso and Modigliani were living at the Bâteau Lavoir in Montmartre). In contrast to his predecessors, however, Modigliani has positioned his sitter frontally, pushing Miestchaninoff's body close to the foreground plane and aligning him with the vertical and horizontal axes of the picture. The hieratic presence of the figure is relieved only by the slight tilt of the head and neck and by the subtle torsion of the shoulders and hips. The positioning of the hands suggests both confidence and a casual awkwardness on the part of the sitter. Miestchaninoff is clad in a blue mechanic's shirt, a garment that was favored by many artists in the Montparnasse circle. In 1916, the same year as the present work, Modigliani painted two portraits depicting the Polish artist Moïse Kisling, one of his closest friends, in a closely comparable pose and similar attire.

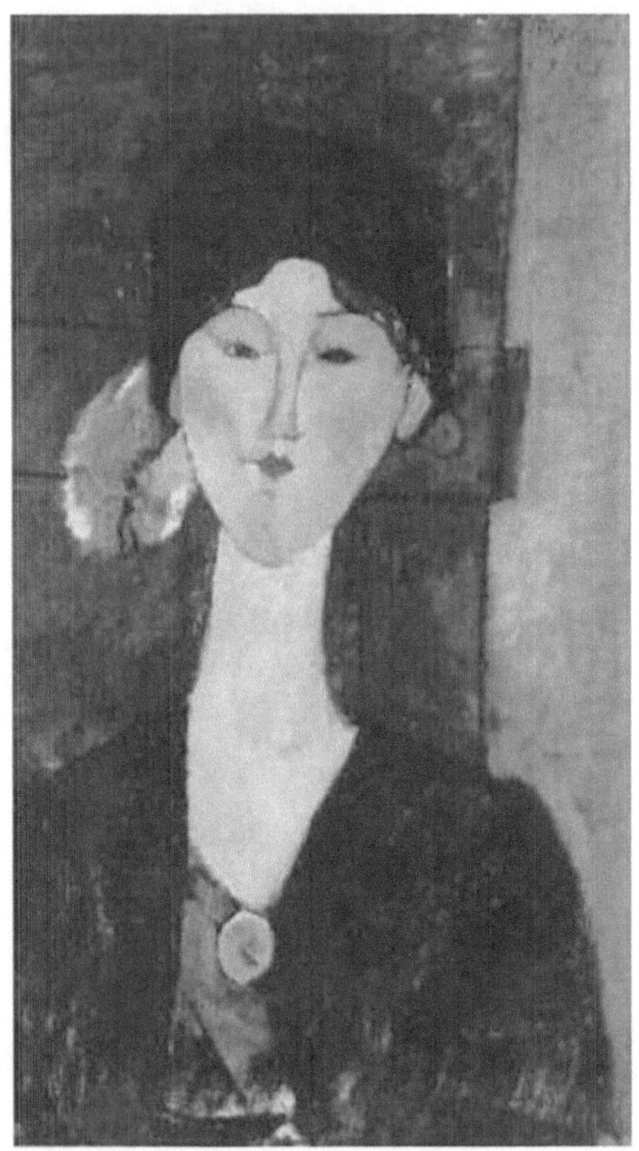

Portrait of Beatrice Hastings,
c. 1916. Oil on canvas. 43 x 27 cm. The Whitehead Collection
(Courtesy Achim Moeller Fine Art, New York

The young woman has pink skin, blonde wavy hair, up-turned nose, and a slightly open mouth. She is motioning outward energetically, a picture of youthful freshness. Modigliani's portrait offers an enchanting peek into the personality of his lover. Beatrice Hastings arrived in Montparnasse in April 1914. She was a poet and correspondent for the English journal New Age. Sculptor Ossip Zadkine introduced the young English woman to Modigliani, who immediately fell in love with her, although their affair was brief. In numerous portraits, the human face and form remained Modigliani's passion for the rest of his short life.

Born Emily Alice Haigh in South Africa in 1879, Beatrice Hastings came to Paris to write a column entitled "Impressions de Paris" for a London literary journal, The New Age. Max Jacob described her as "a great English poet...drunken, musical (a pianist), bohemian, elegant, dressed in the manner of the Transvaal and surrounded by a gang of bandits on the fringe of the arts. The details surrounding the start of Hastings' affair with Modigliani remain uncertain. The sculptor Ossip Zadkine and the English painter Nina Hamnett both claimed to have introduced the pair at the Café Rotonde in Montparnasse, probably in June of 1914. The American sculptor Jacob Epstein is also said to have had a hand in their meeting, according to an anecdote later published in the journal Paris-Montparnasse.

Modigliani's extraordinary portraits of Beatrice Hastings are now housed in major museum collections around the world, including the Barnes Collection, The Art Institute of Chicago, and the Art Gallery of Ontario.

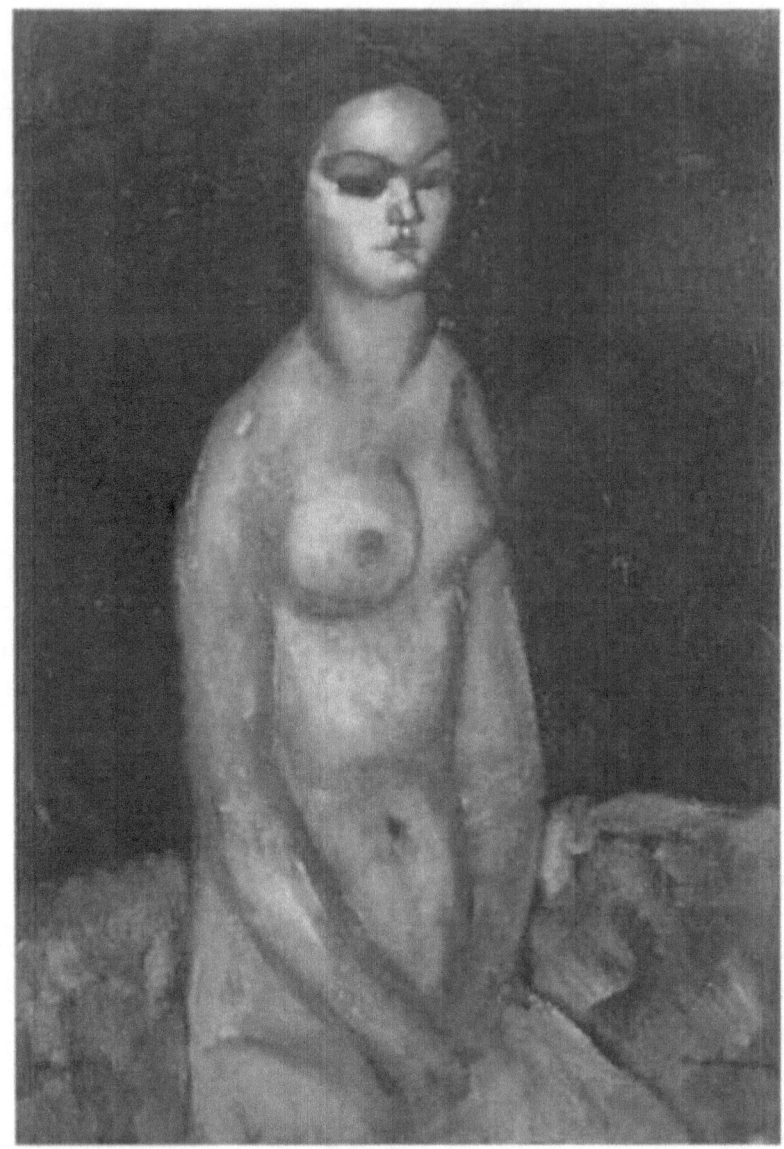

Seated nude
1908. Oil on canvas. 73 x 49.9 cm. Private Collection
Modigliani had painted female nudes from the time of his arrival
in Paris. His first works were notably expressive and conformed to

the Symbolist idea of the female body as a source of sin. Later, his nudes lost this moralizing content and embraced a Mediterranean sensuality.

In 1917 and with the consolidation of his mature style, Modigliani began his popular series of reclining nudes on the request of his friend and new dealer, Léopold Zborowski, who aimed to sell them to collectors interested in the newest type of avant-garde art. However, the thirty or so works painted in Zborowski's apartment between 1917 and 1919 did not meet with the anticipated interest. In these works Modigliani looked to the example of earlier nudes, from Giorgione's Venus to Goya's Naked Maja, flattening the female form in a way first used by Ingres and ultimately adopted by Picasso. Most notable, however, is their erotic charge, which reflects the spirit of sexual liberty prevailing in Montparnasse in the second decade of the century and which shocked many of those who saw these paintings.

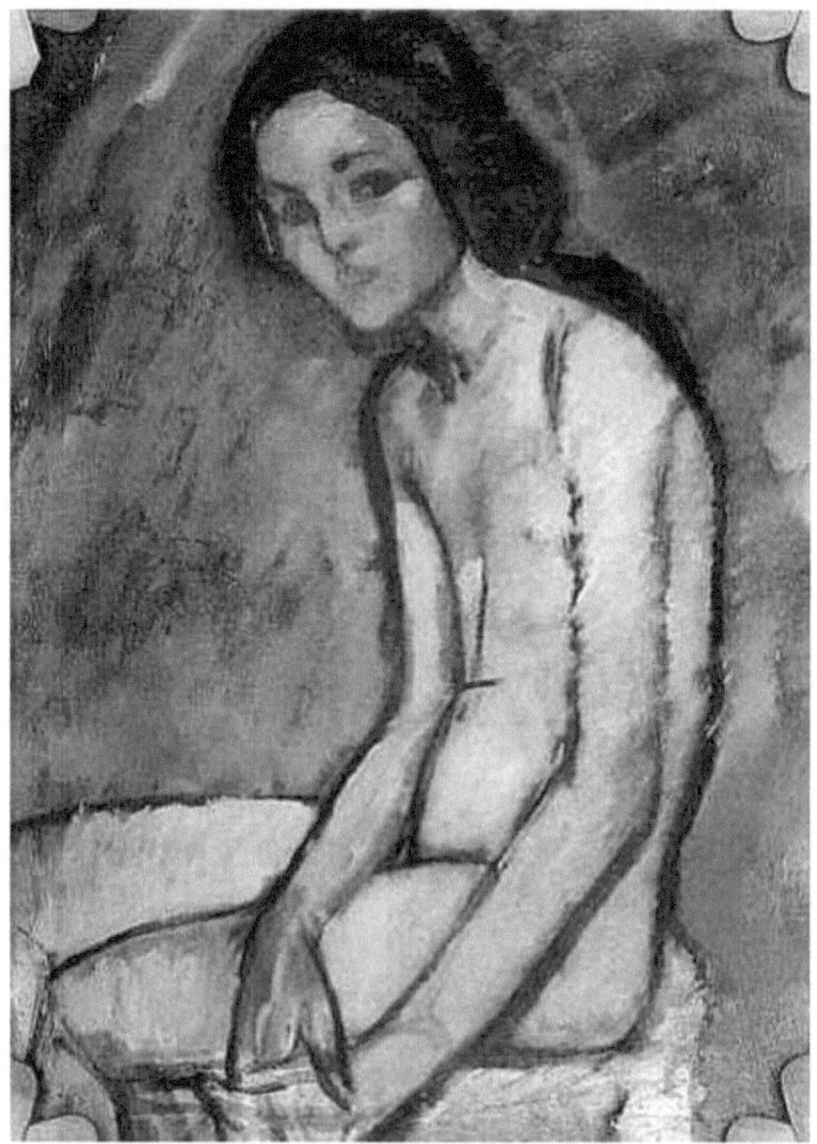

Seated nude
1909. Oil on canvas. Private Collection

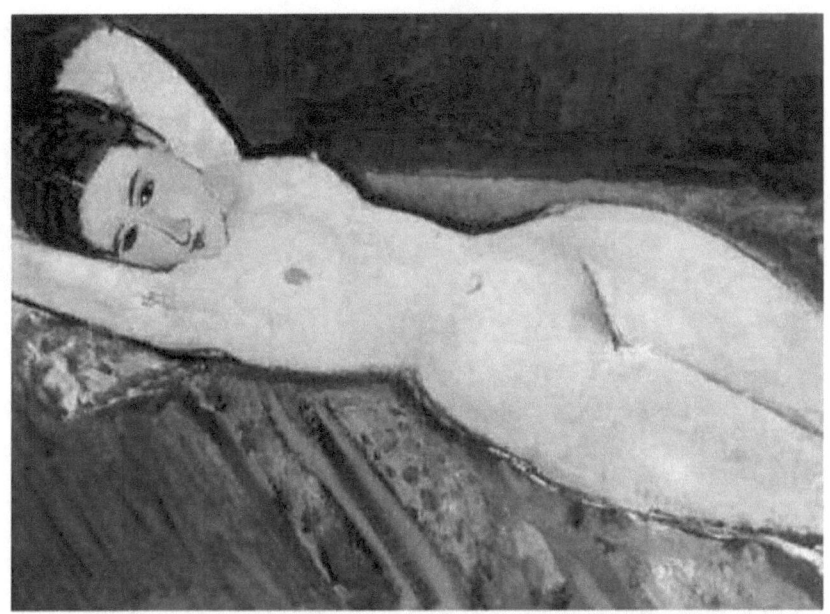

Reclining nude with Arms Folded under Her Head
1916, Oil on canvas, 65.5 x 87 cm, Bührle Collection, Zurich,
Switzerland

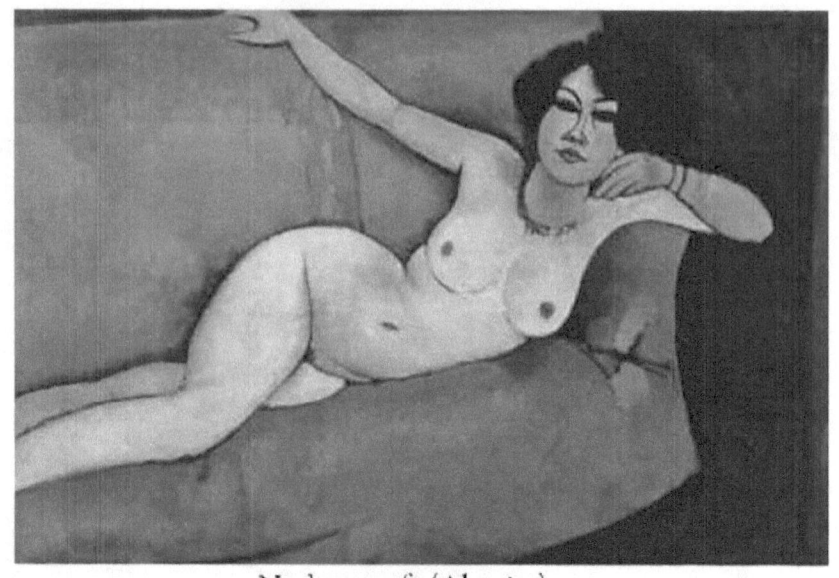

Nude on sofa (Almaisa)
1916, Oil on canvas, 81 x 116 cm, Private Collection

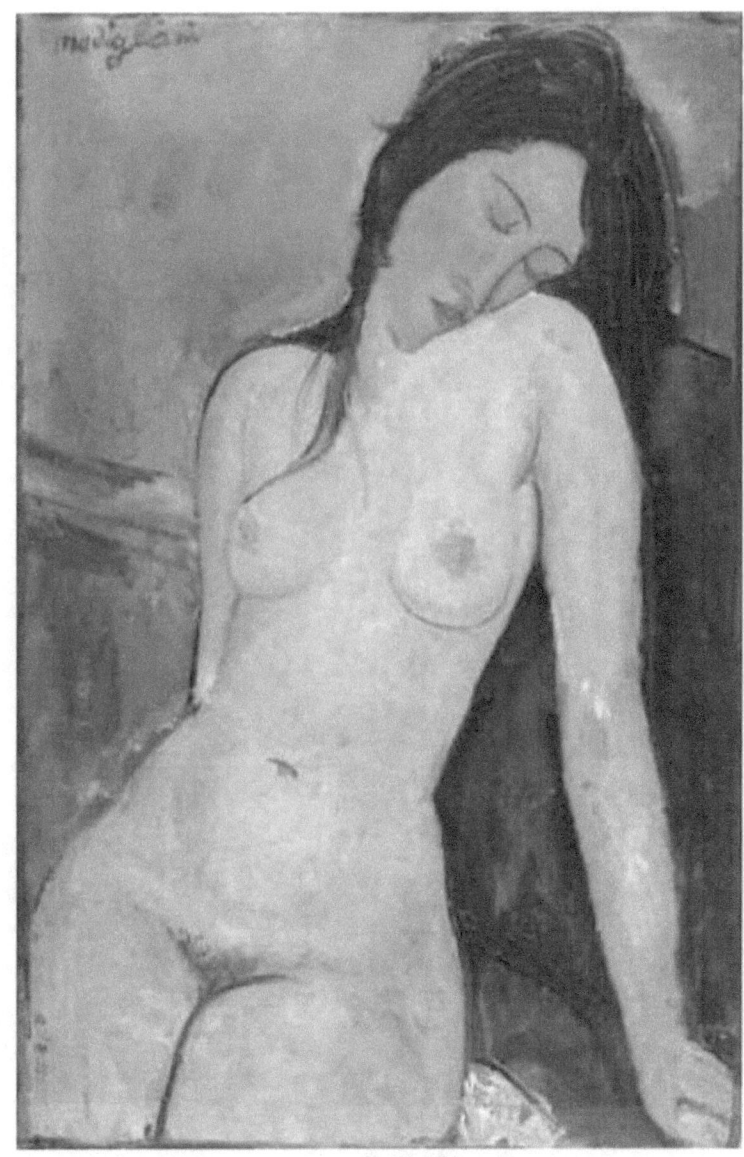

Female Nude
1916. Oil on canvas. 92.4 cm x 59.8 cm. The Courtauld
Gallery. London

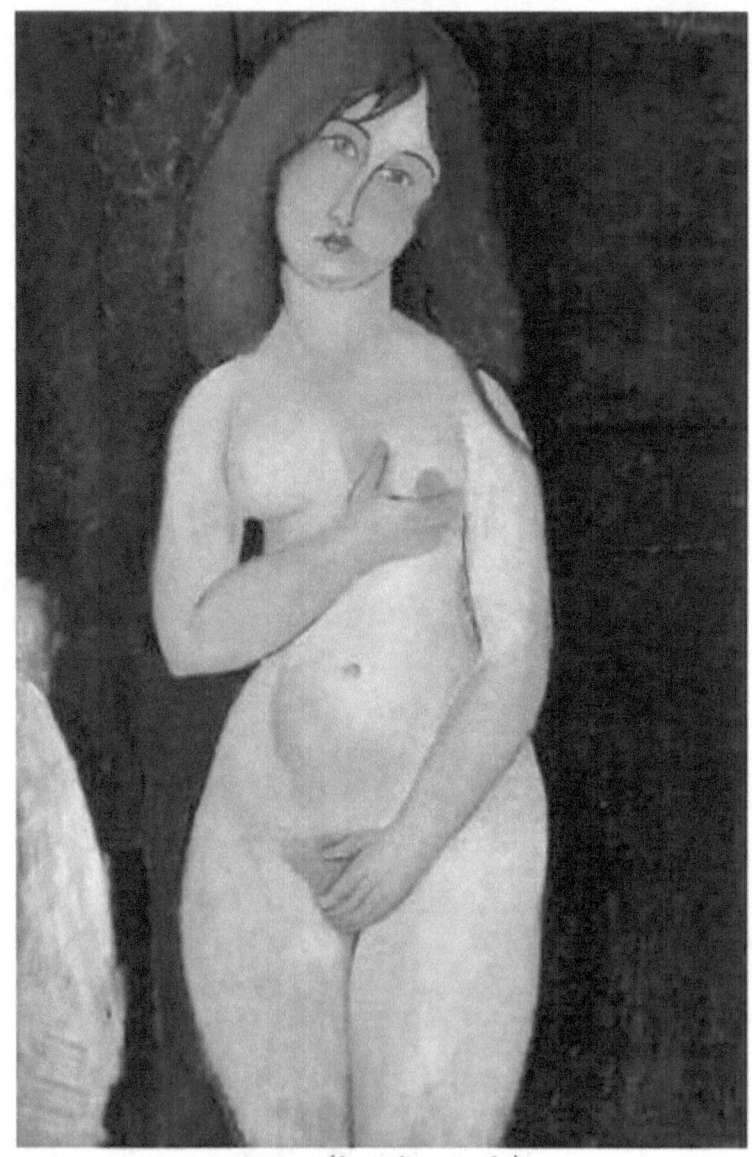

Venus (Standing nude)
1917. Oil on canvas. 99.5 x 84.5 cm. Private Collection

Modigliani recalled from his student days in Florence, wandering about the Uffizi, the Medici Venus, a Roman copy done in the 1st century BC after a classic Greek marble. The Florentine painter Masaccio used this pose in his Expulsion of Adam and Eve, 1422-1426, in which the shamed, sinful Eve attempts to cover her nakedness as she is driven from the Garden of Eden. Botticelli, another Florentine master, revived the gesture of the Medici Venus in its original antique, pagan and sensual context for his famous Birth of Venus, also in the Uffizi.

Apart from his stylized caryatides after antique sources, Modigliani painted only four nudes before 1916. In 1916 Modigliani painted a seated nude and six reclining nudes. At the end of that year Zborowski and his wife moved to an apartment at 3, rue Joseph Bara, where they turned over one of their rooms to Modigliani for use as a studio. It was here that Modigliani painted Vénus, and the other great nudes, twenty in all, of 1917. Zborowski, by the terms of his contract, expected Modigliani to paint nudes. He knew that would they would be more commercially viable than straight portraits, and would offer the painter a challenge that was truly worthy of his talent and skill. Zborowski, in effect, commissioned the series of twenty nudes that Modigliani painted during this time, in some cases for his own collection, or more importantly, for use in his plan to promote the artist. Of the twenty nudes, thirteen are reclining and five are seated. In only two, including Vénus, is the model standing, in three-quarter length. Modigliani employed in them the same broad-hipped girl whose red hair no doubt reminded him of Botticelli's Venus. She appears nowhere else in the series.

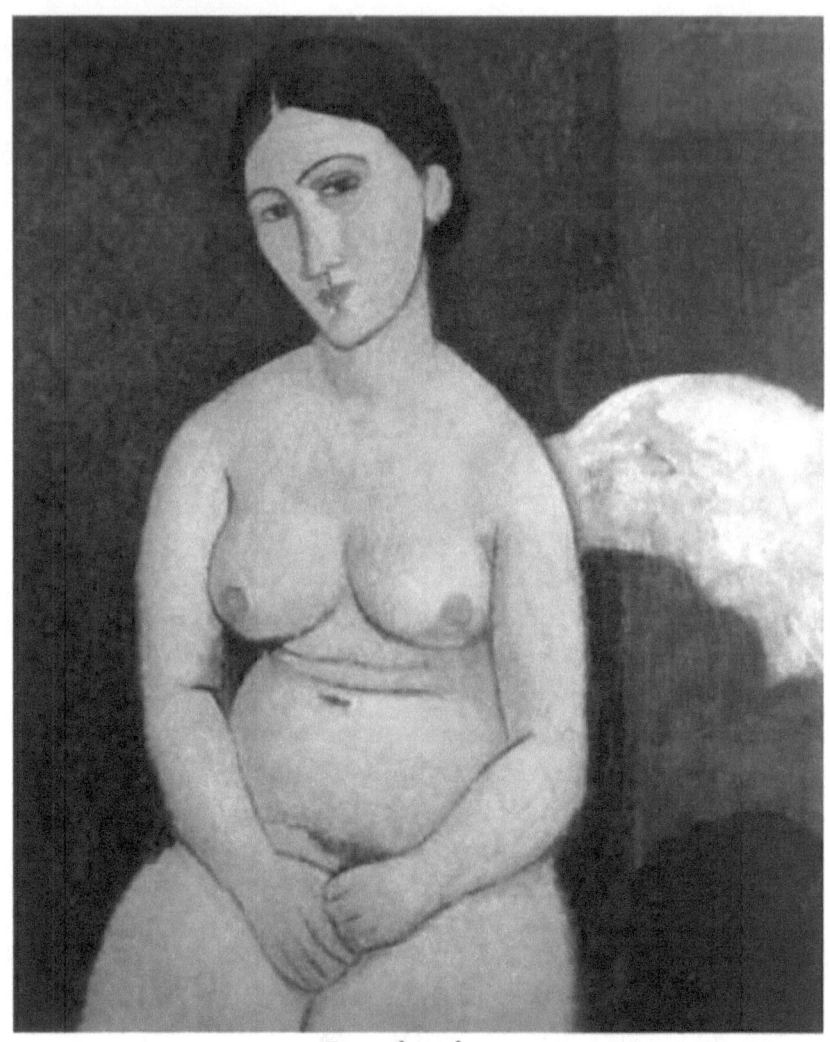

Seated nude
1917, Oil on canvas, 81 x 65 cm, Private Collection

MODIGLIANI

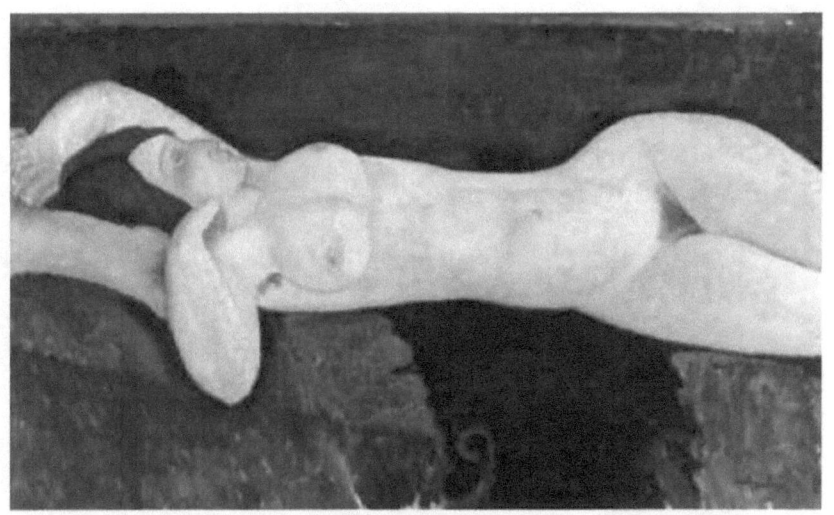

Le grand Nu (The great nude)
1917, Oil on canvas, 73 x 116 cm, Museum of Modern Art,
USA

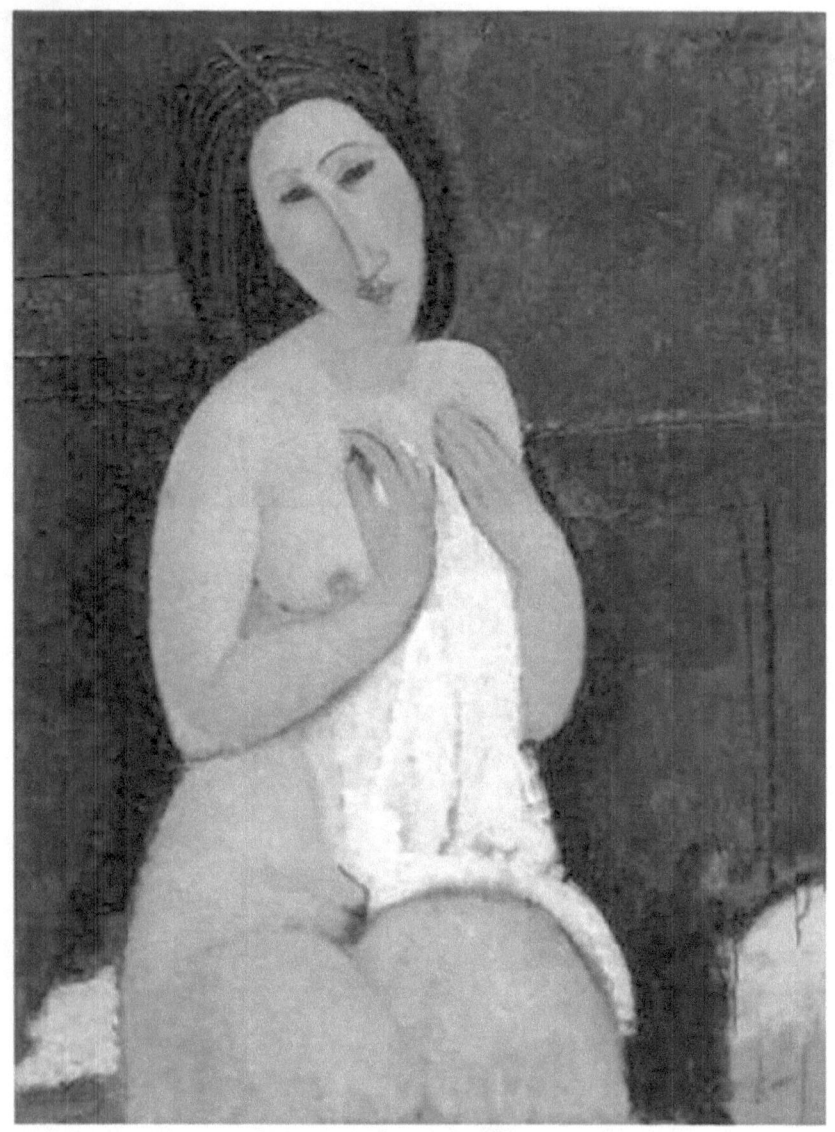

Seated nude with a Shirt
1917. Oil on canvas.92 x 67.5 cm. Musée d'Art moderne. Lille.
France

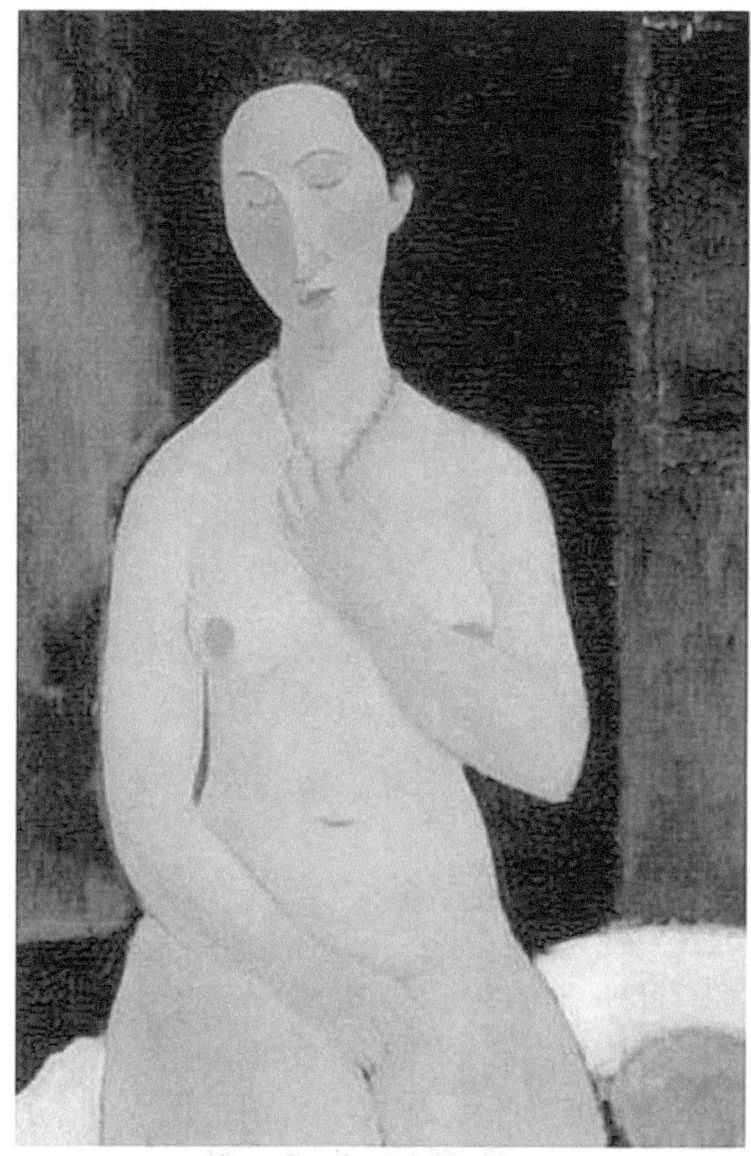

Seated nude with Necklace
1917, Oil on canvas, Private Collection

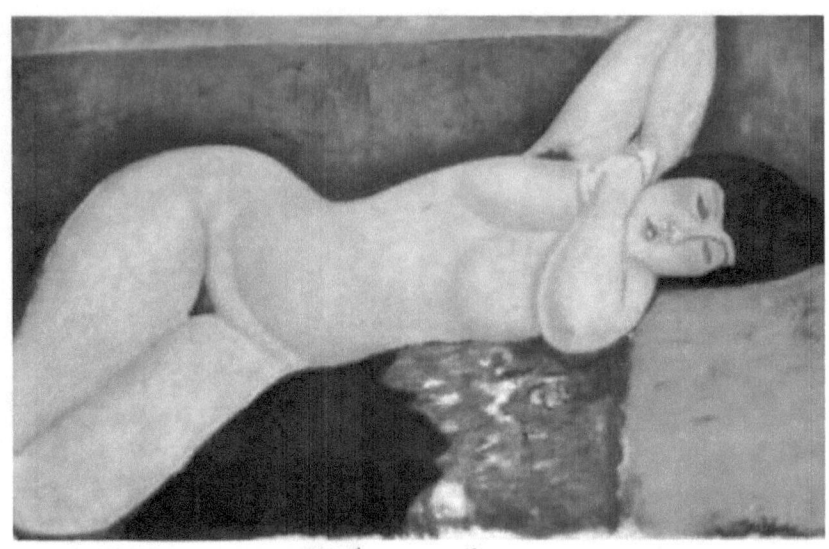

Reclining nude
c.1917, Oil on canvas, 46 x 54 cm, Private Collection

MODIGLIANI

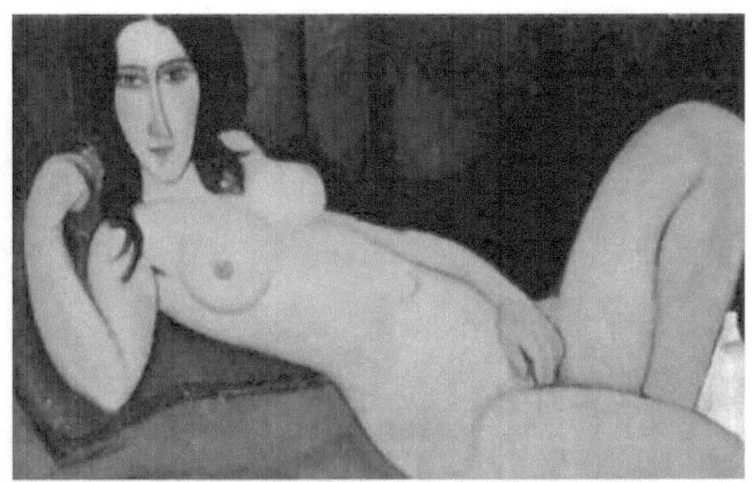

Reclining nude

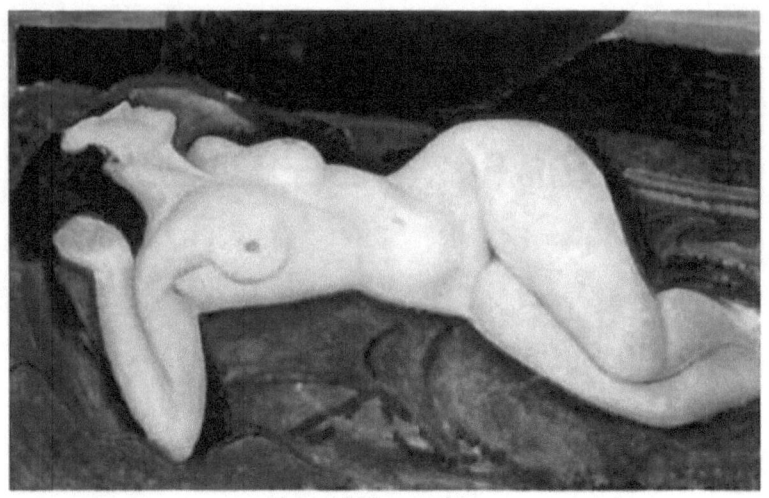

Recumbent nude
c.1917, Oil on canvas, 65 x 100 cm, Private Collection

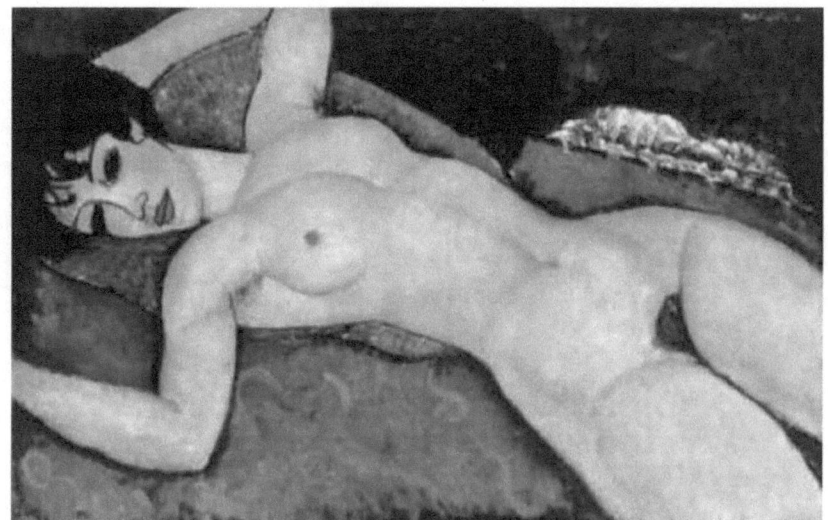

Female Nude Reclining on a White Pillow
1917, Oil on canvas, 60 x 92 cm, Private Collection

In 1917, Modigliani held a one-man exhibition in Paris, which was closed within a few hours by the Paris Chief of Police, who considered the nudes shocking and scandalous. This painting was created in 1917, and thus it may be the culprit behind Modigliani's failure, as it was the only exhibition he ever held. Unlike his other more elongated forms; the nude body of the woman is graciously painted with flowing curves and a sensual texture; the mask-like face with eyes full of mystery, and a slight smile to the lips. It is not so scandalous and shocking as it is a celebration of the woman's form and her sensual nature.

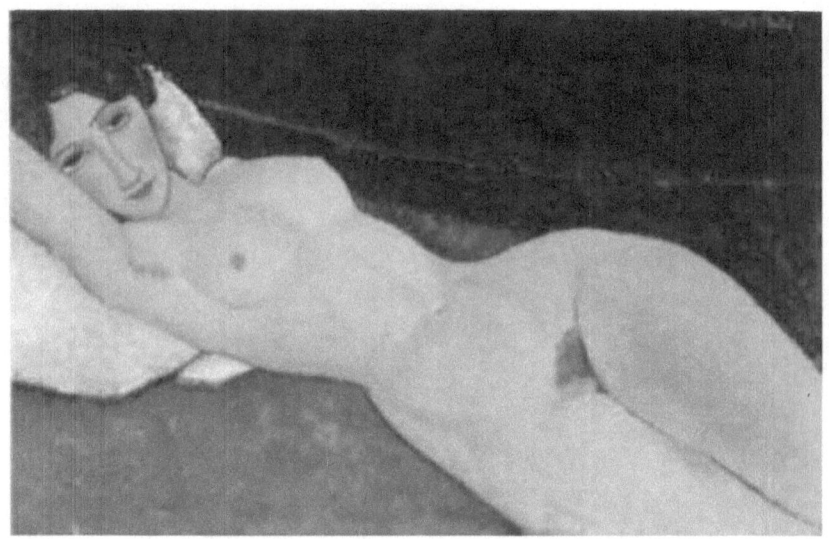

Female Nude Reclining on a White Pillow
1917, Oil on canvas, Staatsgalerie Stuttgart (Germany)
The well-proportioned body stands out strikingly against the lush reddish-brown and bluish-black of the background. The head resting against one arm on the light-colored pillow has a mask like beauty; only the dark, veiled gaze communicates a sense of secrecy and seductiveness. The smoothly modeled appearance of the individual body forms, along with their warm skin tone and the tautly rounded contours, are imbued with a consistent rhythm throughout, as the nude body fills the canvas like a large arabesque.

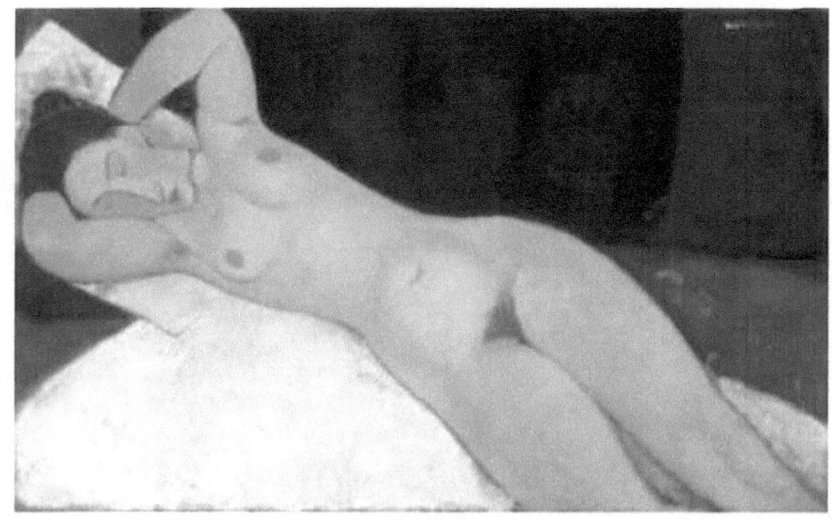

Nude (Nu)
1917. Oil on canvas, 73 x 116.7 cm. Solomon R. Guggenheim
Museum

Modigliani painted this unknown model three times, the other two works show her reclining, one wearing the same necklace but with open eyes and one with closed eyes and hands behind her head.

This work embodies the totality of his vision as an artist in every respect: the rich dark background of black and chocolate brown which throws her illuminated body into strong relief; the three vertical lines in the background (five if we count the edges of the canvas itself) which favor her elongation even though her hips spread abundantly in the horizontal and the soft plump white fabric on which she is perched, rendered in an impasto as rich as that of her thick chestnut hair. Her face, too, is perfection, the features drawn with a few strong swift strokes of great clarity and balance, the contours gently modeled to give depth to the refinement of the almost perfect oval.

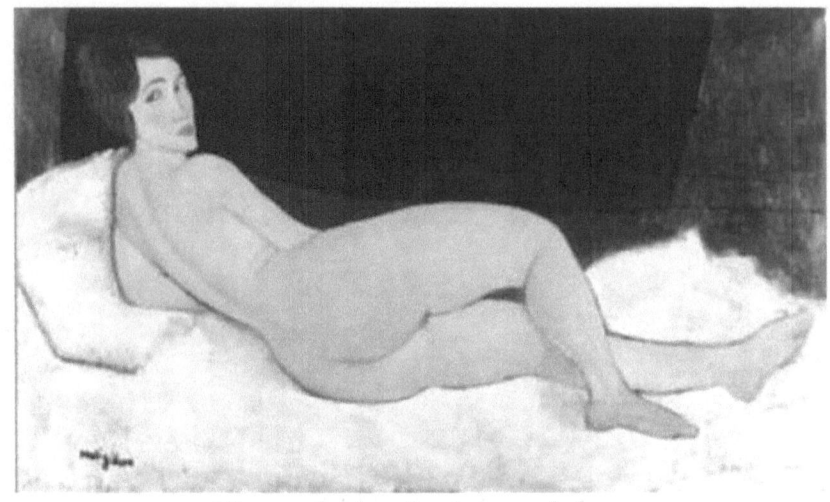

Nu couché (sur le côté gauche)
1917, Oil on canvas, Private Collection

The pose of the present work is in fact closely comparable to that of Ingres's celebrated Grande odalisque, of which a front view, now lost, once existed as a pendant. In both Modigliani's painting and the Grande odalisque, the nude is shown recumbent on her left side, torso propped on one elbow, right calf bent over left, head turned to fix the viewer with a gaze at once placid and coquettish. As in Ingres's masterpiece, Modigliani's languorously reclining nude fills the long, horizontal canvas from left to right, the arc of her back, swell of her buttocks, and graceful curve of her right shoulder articulated with sweeping, sinuous lines. The influence of Ingres upon Modigliani is far from coincidental. By 1917, Ingrisme was a key component of the burgeoning tendency toward neo-classicism among many artists of the Parisian avant-garde, Picasso above all. At the same time, the Grande odalisque, with its subtle anatomical dislocations, had long been seen as evidence of a latent iconoclasm within Ingres's art (witness Picasso's cubist copy of the picture from 1907-1908). This very combination of classicism and innovation in the Grande odalisque had in fact become the topic of widespread discussion in the early years of the century, when

Manet's Olympia was moved from the Musée du Luxembourg to the Louvre and hung alongside Ingres's masterpiece. To some this pairing served to signal the triumph of Manet's modernity, while for others it underscored the formal daring of the older picture. For an artist such as Modigliani, whose nudes are steeped in tradition yet radical in their originality, the appeal of Ingres must have lain in his shrewd negotiation of this same paradox.

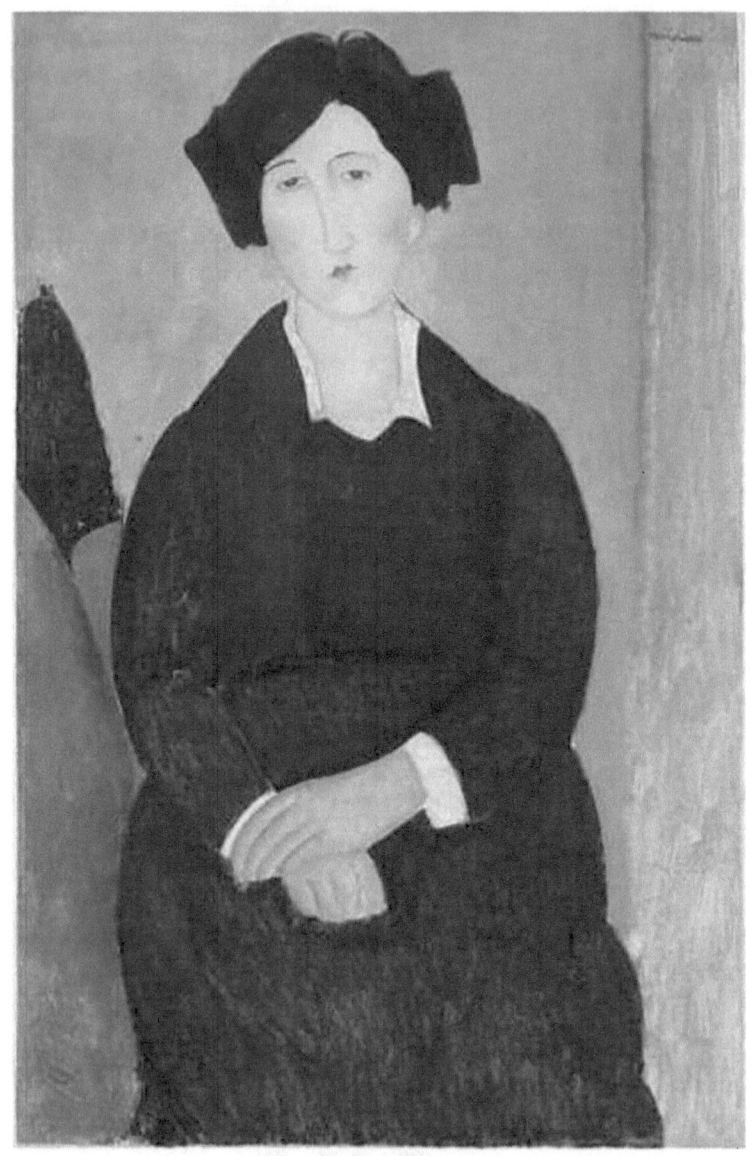

The Italian Woman
1917. Oil on canvas. 102.6 x 67cm. The Metropolitan
Museum of Art

The identity of the patient-looking sitter is unknown. Modigliani might have chosen her because she was a compatriot. Most of the artist's models were not professionals, except those he hired for his pictures of female nudes.

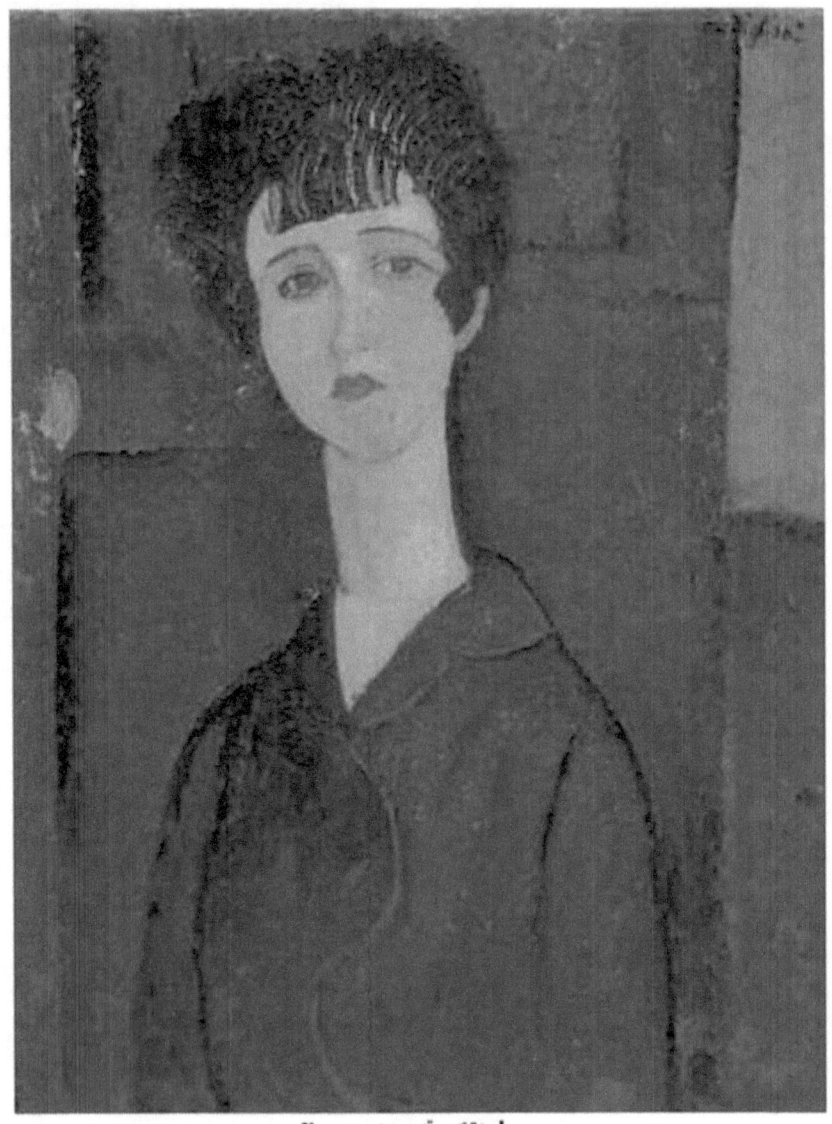

Portrait of a Girl
c.1917, Oil paint on canvas, 80.6 x 59.7 cm, Collection Tate
Bequeathed by C. FrankBy the time Modigliani painted this
portrait he had developed his distinctive style of representing the
figure.

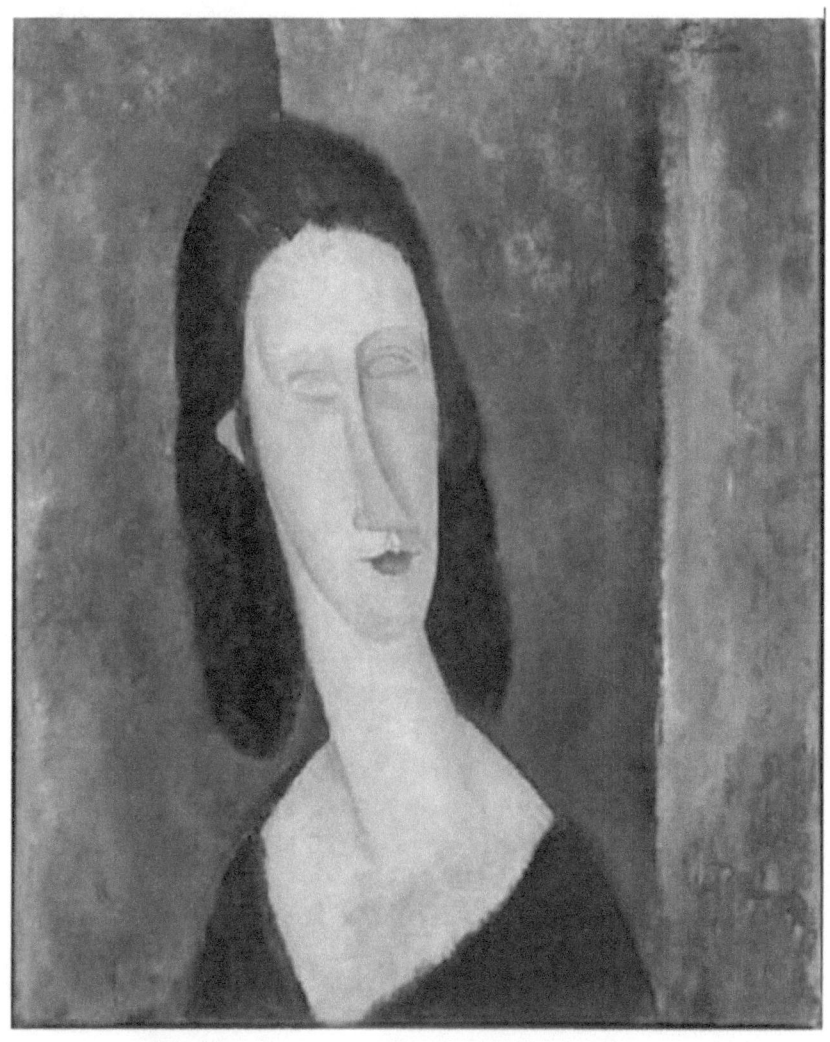

Blue Eyes (Portrait of Madame Jeanne Hébuterne)
1917, Oil on canvas, 54.6 x 42.9 cm, Philadelphia Museum of
Art

MODIGLIANI

Born in Livorno, Italy, on the coast of Tuscany, Modigliani moved to Paris in January 1906, where he quickly fell in with Pablo Picasso, Max Jacob, and the other artists and writers of the Bateau-Lavoir studios in Montmartre. Here his Sephardic-humanist upbringing met with the equally eclectic interests of his peers, giving rise to a distinctive style of portraiture influenced by a wide variety of historical and cultural sources. This elegant portrait of the artist's girlfriend, possibly painted at the Montparnasse apartment that the couple shared from 1917 to 1920, reveals Modigliani's appreciation for Italian Renaissance painting and African sculpture, as well his lasting connection to the Cubist movement.

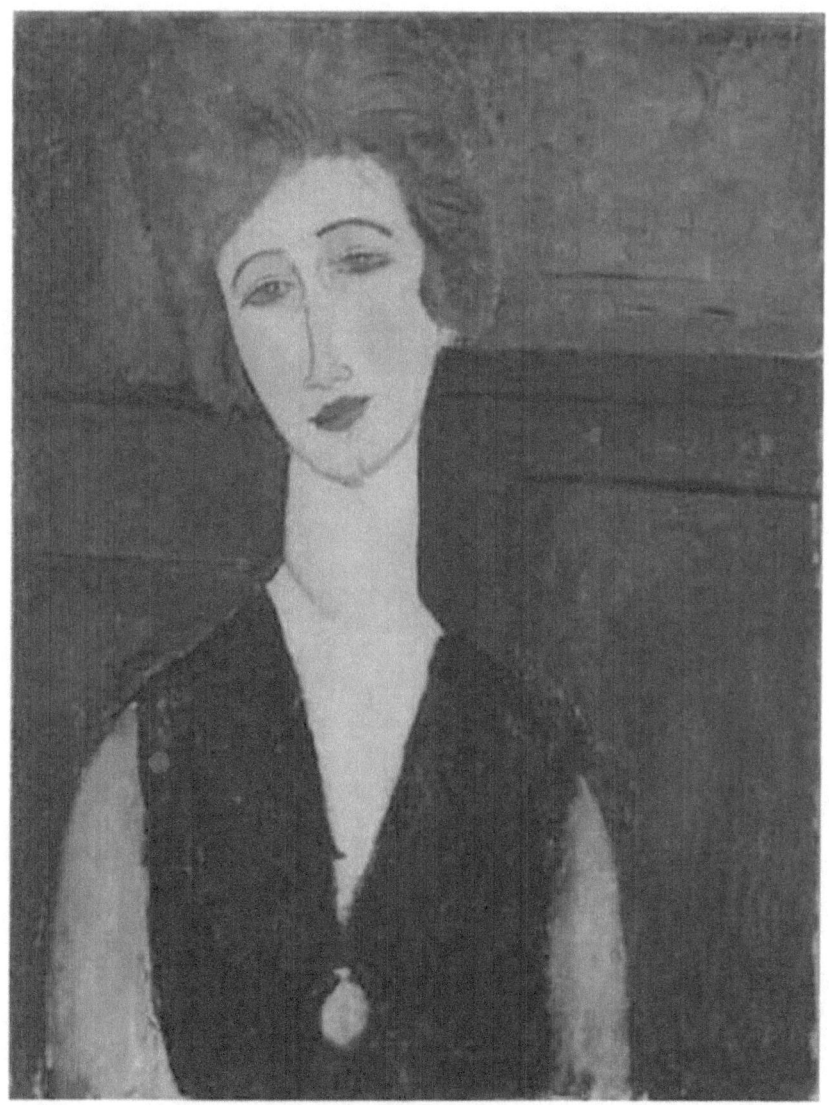

Portrait of a Woman

c.1917-18, oil on canvas, 65 x 48.30 cm, Public Collection
Modigliani studied briefly in Florence and Venice before moving
to Paris in 1906. His portraits chronicle the lives of fellow artists
and poets, although the woman in this painting remains

unidentified. Influenced by African masks and Cubism, he rendered her features as flat, geometric planes. The gracefully elongated neck and nose may also derive from the Renaissance paintings of Sandro Botticelli and Parmigianino, thereby elegantly merging Western and non-Western, modern and traditional styles.

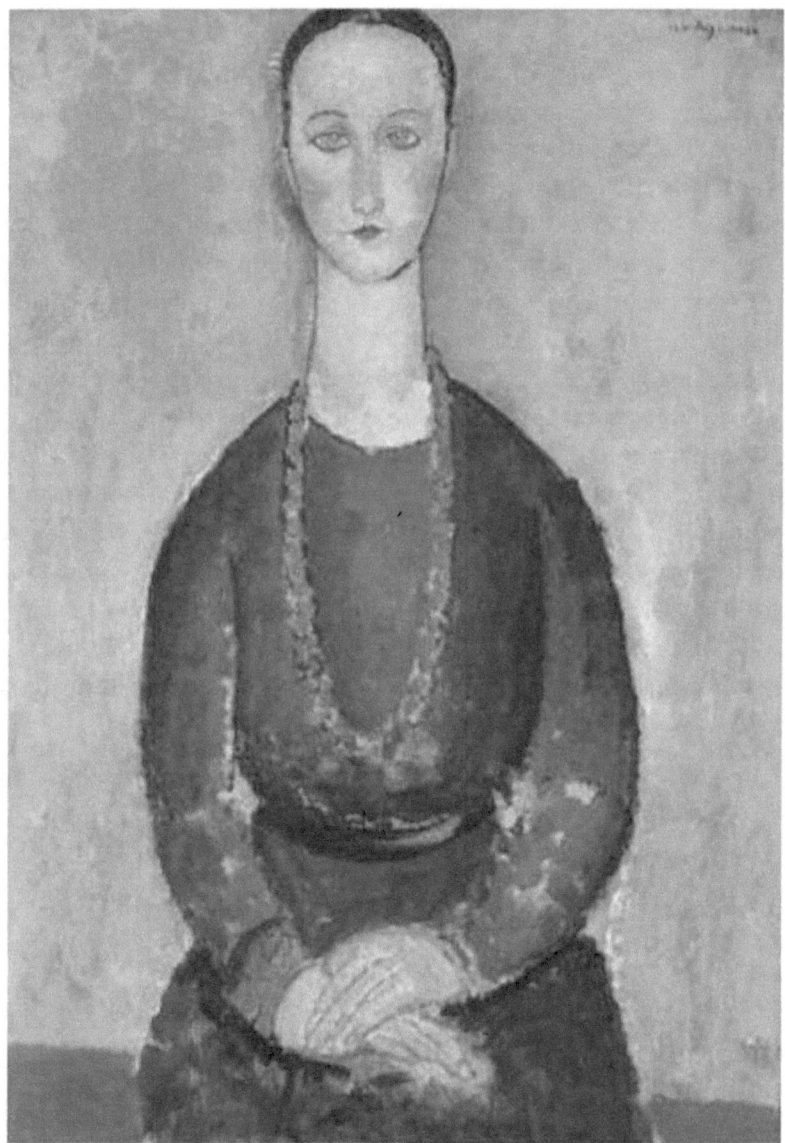

Donna con collana rossa (Woman with red necklace)
1918, oil on canvas, 92.5 x 65.3 cm. Private Collection

The present painting epitomizes this new approach to portraiture.
It depicts a young woman, no longer an adolescent but only

recently an adult. Her name is recorded as either Madeleine Verdon or Madeleine Verdou, but nothing else about her is known; she was presumably one of the residents of Cagnes whom Modigliani engaged to pose for him in 1918-1919. At first glance, she seems the epitome of passivity and calm, her hands clasped in her lap, her face expressionless. Certain details of the composition, however, belie this initial impression. The girl's face, for instance, is more heavily worked than the remainder of the painting, serving to focus the viewer's attention on her inscrutable features and suggesting the richness of feeling that they mask. The outlines of the figure waver slightly, producing a sensation of energy and potential kinesis; this is heightened by the fact that juncture of the wall and floor behind the sitter is off-axis. The colors in the painting also contribute to the impression of tension and vibration, with the bright red of the girl's necklace and bracelet forming a strong contrast to the deep navy of her dress and the pale blue of the background. Reddish-pink dots outline her fingers as well, suggesting that her clasped hands are meant to imply energy and restlessness rather than quietude and repose.

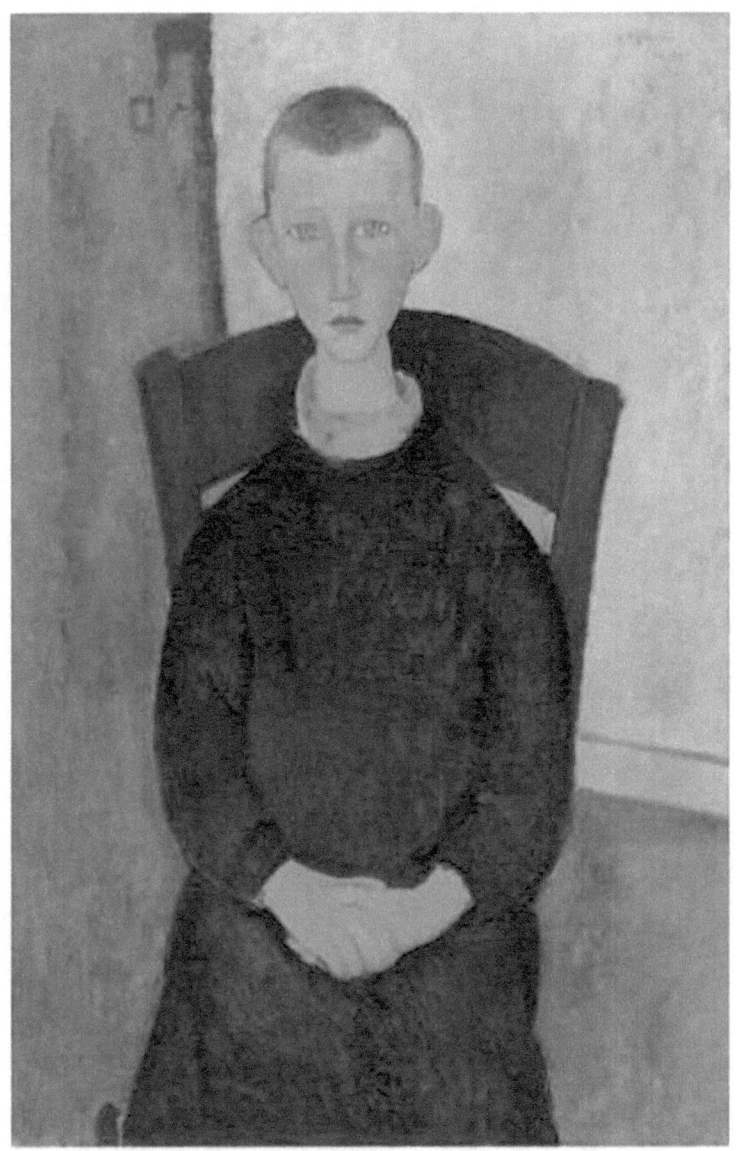

Le Fils du Concierge (The son of the concierge)
1918, oil on canvas, 92 × 60 cm, Private Collections
Among the pictures which Modigliani made at Cagnes is a group
of paintings depicting the children of the concierge of his villa.

MODIGLIANI

Modigliani, like so many Italians, was extremely sensitive to children. Lionello Venturi has suggestively described his late portraits of them: At this time, Modigliani's attitude towards and the depiction of his models became calmer and more peaceful. The apprentice, the porter's son, the maid in Cagnes, little Maria, the two girls in Paris, all enter Modigliani's pictorial world with a sad dignity. Their interior vision, captured in a private dream, accentuates their solitude and at the same time enshrines their morality with a poetic halo. Their status in life is certainly not a happy one, but they possess nobility and moral values.

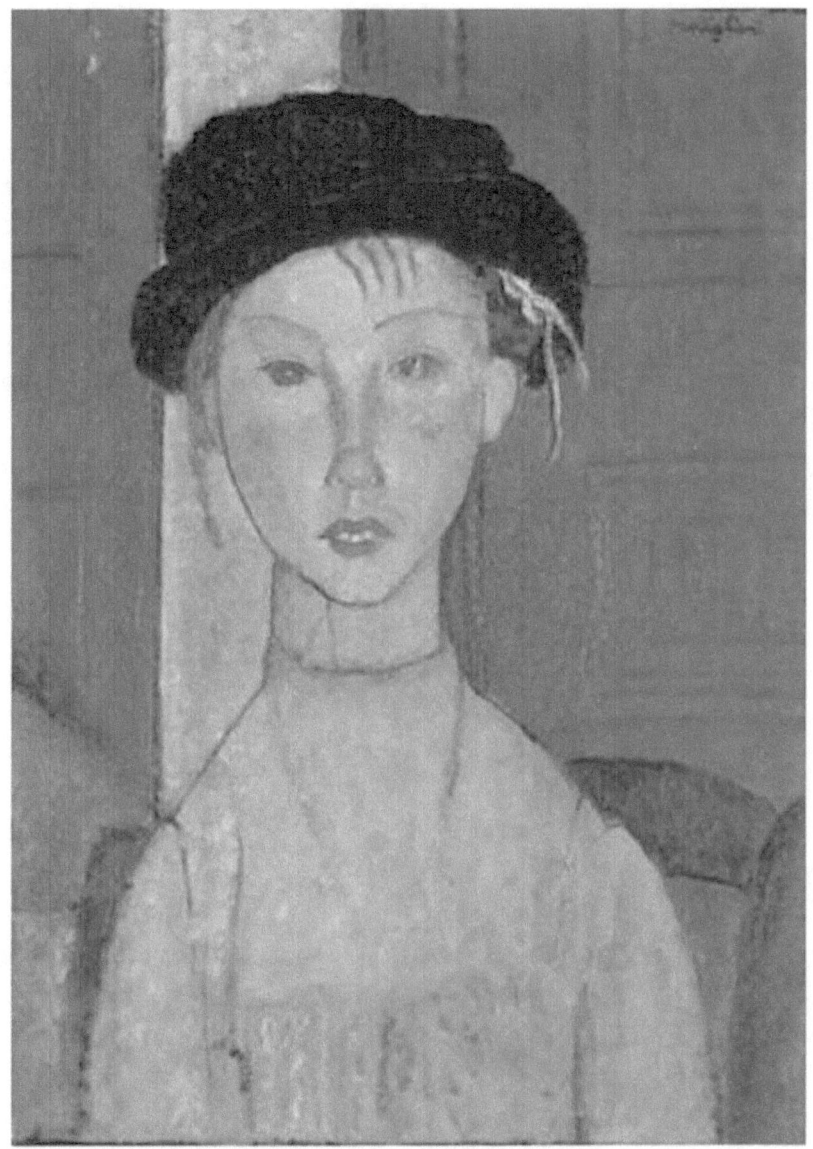

Jeune fille au béret (Girl in beret)
1918, oil on canvas, 65.4 x 46.3 cm, Private Collection
Jeune fille au béret is a striking portrait of a youth whose gaze
appears to sear through the viewer.

MODIGLIANI

Modigliani's portraiture was the result of his long-standing search for harmony, for a visual window into the soul. He was attempting to capture the essence not only of his sitters, but of humanity itself. The faces in his pictures are often likened to masks, and it is a tribute to the skill and unique vision of the painter that in his portraits, these masks make the viewer all the more aware of the spirit that lies beneath them, and which appears to spill forth from the eyes. In Jeune fille au béret, the eyes are rendered in a penetrating, pure blue reminiscent of Modigliani's pictures of his partner, Jeanne Hébuterne, painted during the same period. The blue spills beyond the iris, into the area that would in reality appear as the white, and this heightens the sense that these eyes are windows into the soul of the sitter.

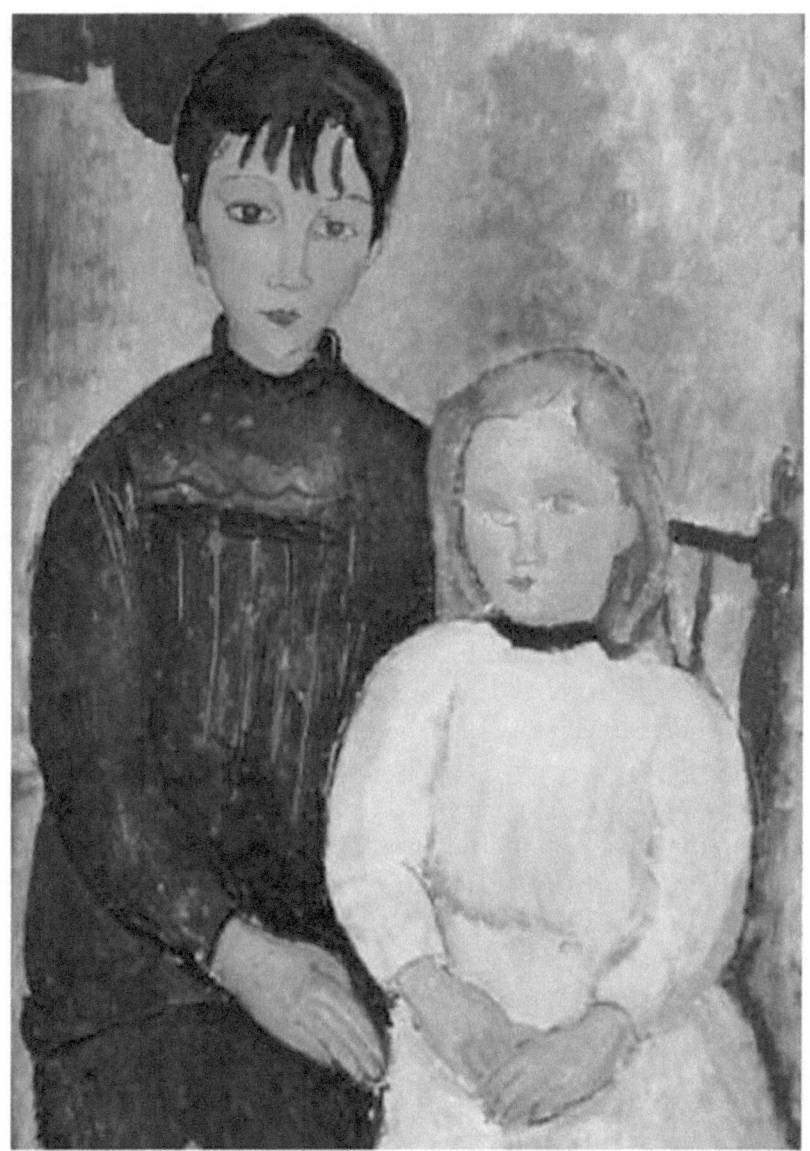

Les deux filles (The two girls)
1918. Oil on canvas. 100.2 x 65.1 cm. Private Collection
Les deux filles is one of only five known double portraits painted
by Modigliani. Throughout his entire oeuvre. Modigliani generally

dedicated himself to the isolated figure, exploring no other problem of composition other than a lone human being viewed face to face. For the most part, it was enough for the artist's intense observation of individual characterization to engage with a single model, yet his rare ventures into multiple figure arrangements are remarkable for their insight into human relationships and the energy communicated by different identities. Of Modigliani's five double portraits, two are portraits of bridal couples, the highly stylized Les époux of 1915 and the celebrated portrait of his close friend, the sculptor Jacques Lipchitz and his wife Bertha (1916). These works celebrate the union between woman and man, whilst Modigliani's other double portraits would address the theme of mother and child (Femme assise avec un enfant, 1919 and Gitane avec un enfant, 1918) - pictures that owe much to Modigliani's Italian inheritance and his enduring love of the early Renaissance masters. Les deux filles is a tender and perceptive painting that explores the connection between two young girls, possibly sisters, whom Modigliani has described in a refined visual language that is both compellingly subjective and intuitive.

Les deux filles is preserved in its original unlined condition and clearly displays Modigliani's virtuoso feeling for paint. His obsession for refining his subjects into simple, interlocking curvilinear forms is evident in the pentimenti visible below the hands of the younger child, where pencil lines chart out his method of perfecting the composition. Modigliani's handling of pigment varies across the canvas, from the thin scumbled brushwork used to diffuse the variegated hues of the background to the highly viscous textures on the figures and chair, the painting manifests a passionate involvement with the qualities and possibilities of his materials and represents the height of his technical development.

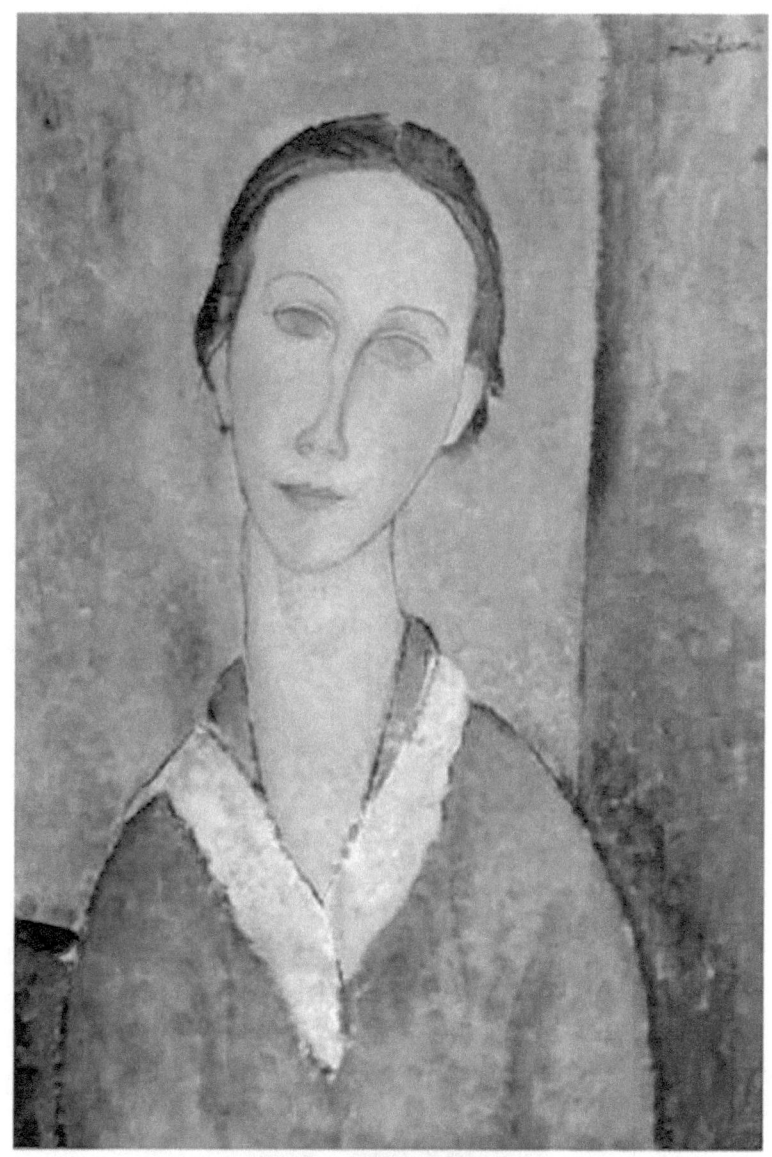

Girl in a Sailor's Blouse
1918. Oil on canvas. 60.3 x 46.4 cm. The Metropolitan
Museum of Art

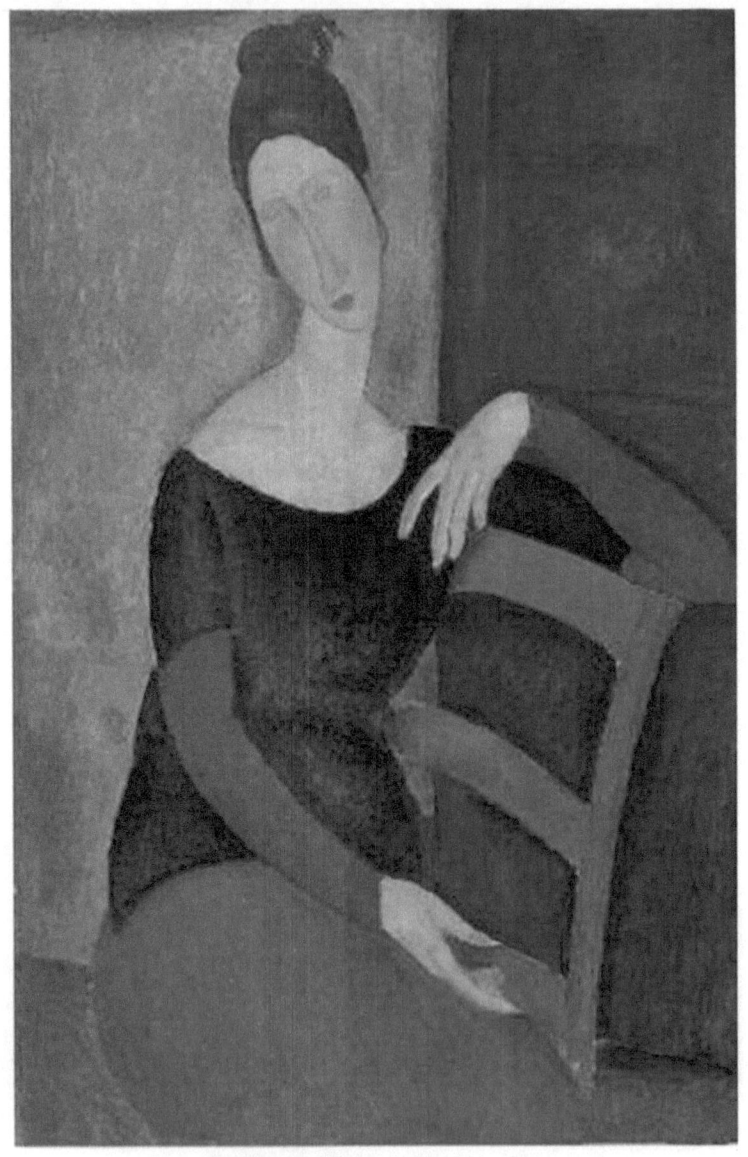

Portrait of the Artist's Wife, Jeanne Hebuterne,
1918, Oil on canvas, 101 x 65.7 cm, Norton Simon Art
Foundation

This is one of the latest depictions of his wife (1898–1920), whose soft features and quiet gaze are not easily distinguishable from the dozens of other three-quarter and bust-height portraits he completed. Stricken with tuberculosis and prone to abusing alcohol and drugs, Modigliani died at age 36, less than two years after this portrait was completed. Bereft, Jeanne killed herself two days later. She was pregnant with their second child.

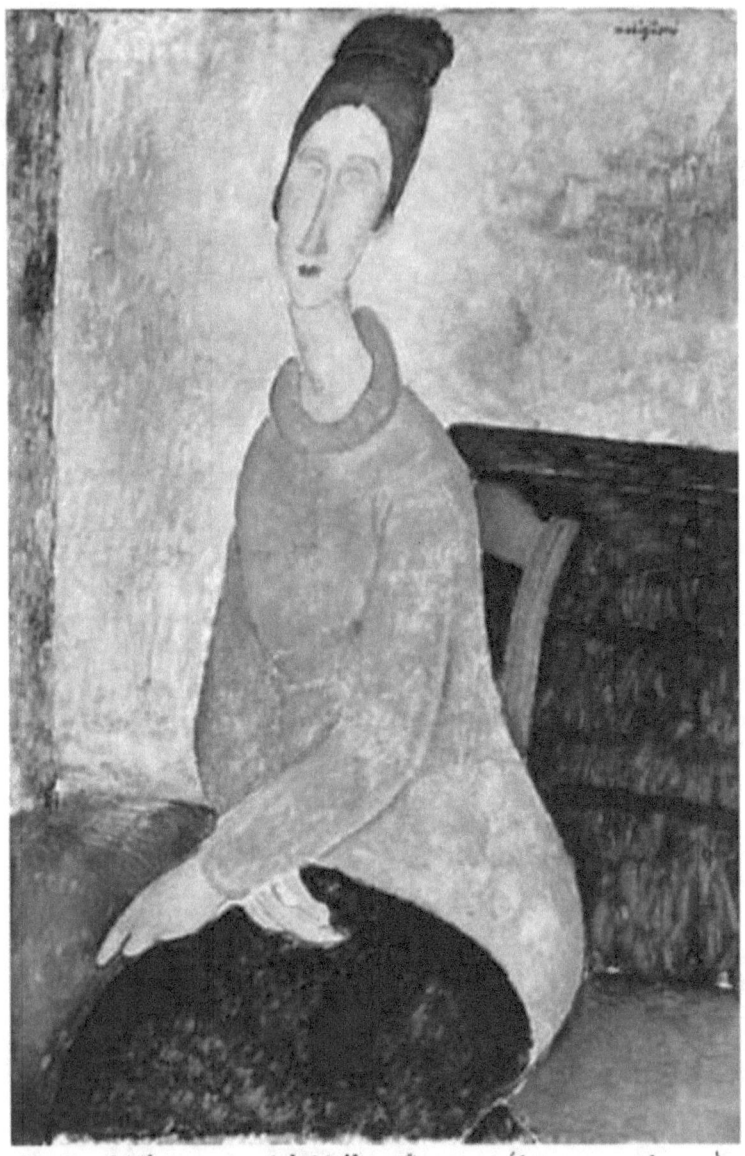

Jeanne Hébuterne with Yellow Sweater (Le sweater jaune), 1918–19. Oil on canvas, 100 x 64.7 cm. Solomon R. Guggenheim Museum, New York

Modigliani's sculptural concerns were translated into paint in Jeanne Hébuterne with Yellow Sweater, in which he portrayed his young companion as a kind of fertility goddess. With her highly stylized narrow face and blank eyes she has the serene countenance of a deity, and the artist's emphasis on massive hips and thighs mimics the focus of ancient sculptures that fetishize reproduction. Both this work and Nude, with their simplified, elongated oval faces, gracefully attenuated noses, and button mouths, suggest the artist's interest in African masks.

Modigliani died of tuberculosis and complications probably brought on by substance abuse and hard living. The tragic fact that Jeanne Hébuterne, pregnant with their second child, committed suicide the next day has only contributed to the infusion of romantic speculation concerning Modigliani's work.

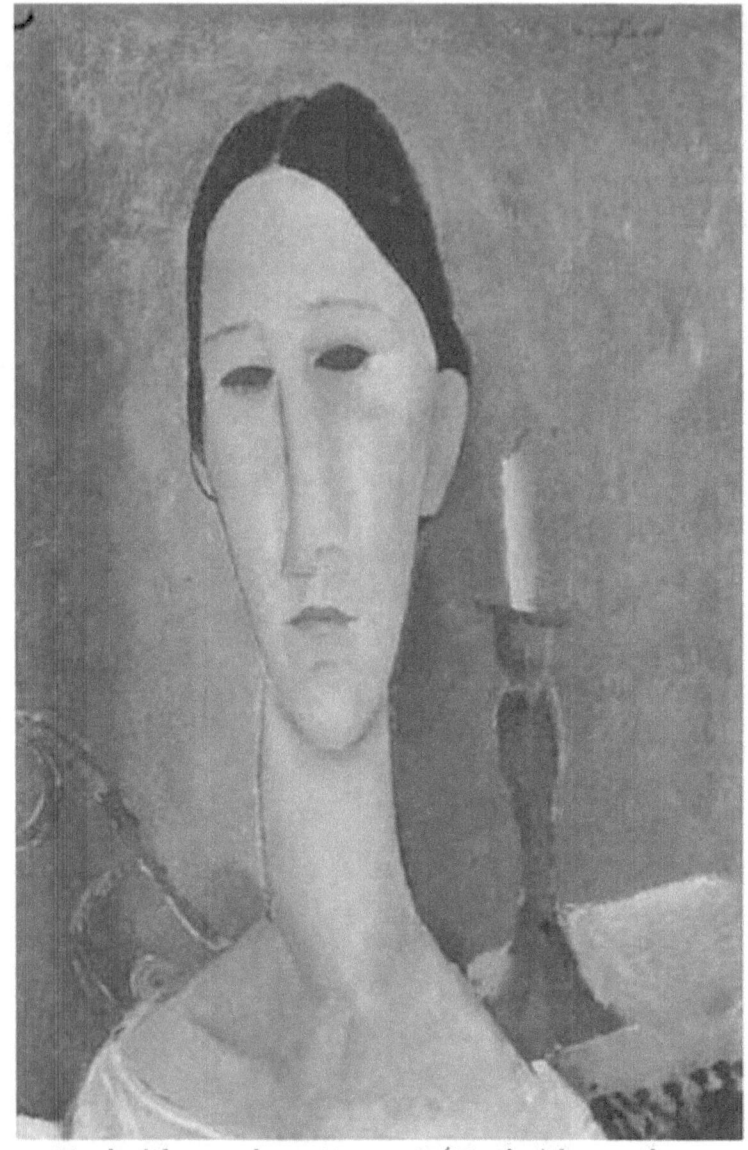

Hanka Zborowska au Bougeoir (Hanka Zborowska at
Candlestick)
1919. Oil on canvas. 46.3 x 29.5cm. Private Collection

Hanka Zborowska, the sitter for this tender and intimate portrait, was the daughter of an old Polish aristocrat who had come to Paris with her husband, Modigliani's friend and dealer, the poet Leopold Zborowski. Zborowski had taken over the management of Modigliani's affairs from Paul Guillaume during 1917, and, unlike the cynical and worldly-wise Guillaume, devoted his energies to furthering the artist's career by searching for suitable models and studios as well as portrait commissions and rich patrons. Modigliani's bohemian manners and life style were profoundly shocking to the refined and aristocratic Hanka. She, however, tolerated his behavior because she recognized his genius and also because she realized that he and other painters, such as Chaim Soutine whom she described as smelling strongly of the abattoirs where he spent so much time working, were important for the success of her husband's career as an art dealer. Together the Zborowskis did their best to support the painter both materially and morally. He often stayed in their apartment in the rue Joseph Bara where they cared for him on the many occasions when he was ill. Hanka became in the end, one of Modigliani's most frequent sitters although the relationship between them always remained reserved and cautious. This emotional distance which existed between the two of them is evident in all the portraits of Hanka that Modigliani painted and the present work, although more tender than most, is no exception.

Many of Modigliani's sitters are presented without any of the humanizing clutter of their surroundings which is visible in the present work. Here the artist has attempted to soften the coolness and reserve of Hanka by including the arc of her chair to the left and by placing her next to a table with its patterned cloth at which he has set the candlestick and candle.

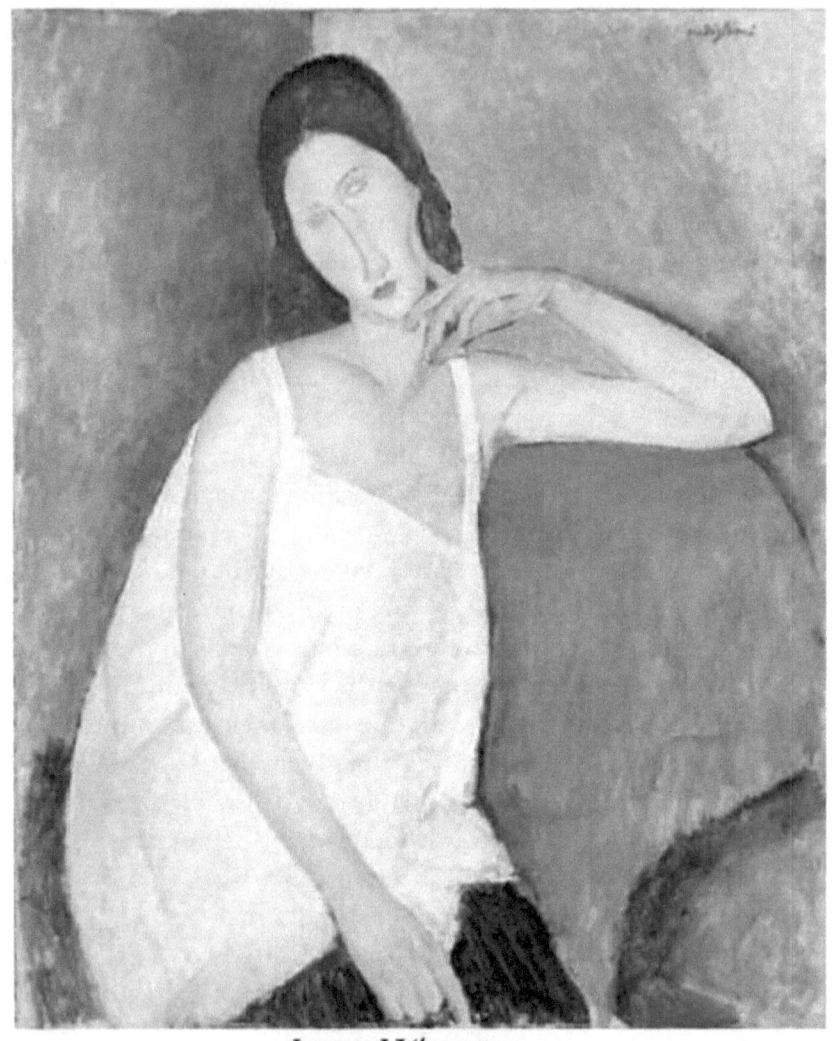

Jeanne Hébuterne
1919, Oil on canvas, 91.4 x 73 cm, The Metropolitan Museum
of Art
Modigliani depicted his mistress, Jeanne Hébuterne (1898-1920),
in more than twenty works but never in the nude. Her casual
white chemise suggests modesty while also hiding her pregnancy.

When Modigliani died from tuberculosis in 1920, Jeanne committed suicide the following day.

www.ingramcontent.com/pod-product-compliance
Lightning Source LLC
Chambersburg PA
CBHW020918180526
45163CB00007B/2791